PRAISE FOR A
HEALING IS KI

"I tried to read this book slowly, but I had to force myself to put it down. It is such a heartfelt and compelling memoir. Gabrielle gives an open and honest account of what her healing journey has been and continues to be. I am amazed at her courage and willingness to change and grow at every stage. This is a must read for anyone on a journey of self-discovery and transformation."

—Allison Post
author of *The Gut Wellness Guide: The Power of Breath, Touch, and Awareness to Reduce Stress, Aid Digestion, and Reclaim Whole-Body Health*

"A powerful cautionary tale—part memoir, part spiritual journey—*All This Healing is Killing Me* gives the reader a front-row seat to what it really takes to be a "spiritual warrior." There are no easy answers, no sudden enlightenment—just the "boots on the ground" hard work of becoming whole. This is a must-read for anyone who is serious about healing—and serious about embarking on a spiritual path."

—Maia Danziger
author of *Relax & Write*

"*All This Healing is Killing Me* shows us how the path to healing and enlightenment can be tortuous, hard. work. Most importantly, we see that, when it comes to emotional pain, we can run, but we can't hide. Not all of us have the courage to stop, turn, and face our pain head on. Thank goodness Gabrielle is a fighter—and a writer—with the courage to do just that."

—Nicholas Garnett
author of In the *Pink: A Memoir*

"*All This Healing is Killing Me* is both an exposé and tribute to anyone who had to climb up hill, down hill, around the hill, and through the center of the damn hill in order to heal back to ourselves after life tried to bury us alive. You won't be able to stop turning the pages and staring at the strength of the human spirit that lives in the author, Gabby Pelicci—as you rediscover and appreciate the indomitable strength that lives in you. Don't miss the experience this book offers for you to encounter the bravest parts of you that have made it through the hardest parts of life. This book is not only a gift, divinely intersected with you for your healing path, but is an anthem for you to keep going."

—Stacey Robbins
author of *God Loves Me, I Think... Stories from Hell, Heaven, and the Other Side of Texas*

"This is a riveting read. Memoirs are interesting, as they are at once deeply personal AND you can find universal truths in them. In *All This Healing is Killing Me*, you are quite likely to find parts that strongly resonate with your own experience of life, which is nicely comforting and enlightening. At the end of the day, we are all on this earth to help heal each other. Thank you to Gabrielle for sharing your story in such an incredible way and lending your voice to the tapestry of the human story."

—Tanya Pergola, Ph.D.
author of *Time is Cows: Timeless Wisdom of the Maasai*

ALL THIS HEALING IS KILLING ME

A Memoir

GABRIELLE PELICCI, PH.D.

MANHATTAN
BOOK GROUP

Published by Manhattan Book Group
447 Broadway | 2nd Floor #354 | New York, NY 10013 | USA
1.800.767.0531 | www.manhattanbookgroup.com

Printed in the United States of America
ISBN: 978-1-960142-90-0

GABRIELLE PELICCI, PH.D.

ALL THIS HEALING IS KILLING ME

Gabrielle Pelicci, Ph.D. "Dr. Gabby" is a professor and coach, guiding individuals and groups towards wholeness using writing as medicine. She completed her doctoral work in Transformative Studies at the California Institute of Integral Studies, with additional degrees in Psychology and Educational Technology from Columbia University. During her 20+ year career, Dr. Gabby has taught hundreds of students and clients proven strategies for positive change in life and work. She specializes in creating wellbeing at the intersection of Integrative Health, Spirituality and Storytelling.

AUTHOR'S NOTE

In writing this book, I've recounted my memories as best I can. Everything that I write is my truth, as honestly as I can tell it. Out of courtesy, I've changed some names and identifying attributes. I have recreated dialogue as closely as I can remember it. This story is personal and told from my point of view. No doubt, others may have a different version, but I have tried to be as accurate as possible based on the experiences as I remember them.

> **Warning**: this book is intended for adults and contains abuse, addiction, death, domestic violence, eating disorders, mental illness, sexual situations, suicide, and trauma. Please take care of yourself while reading the book.

NOBODY TELLS YOU HOW to become an adult. There are no rites of passage, no ceremonial vision quests, or mentoring by wise elders. Moving from adolescence to adulthood, I felt as unsteady as I did as a fashion model walking in 4-inch pumps on the runway. I was a hot mess. I longed to know my purpose and what I was here to do or be, but I didn't have a clue how to discover that. It didn't help that the people who raised me had few redeeming qualities, and the culture and media surrounding me was prompting me to be somebody I was not.

I knew all the things that I didn't want to be. I didn't want to be drunk and violent. I dreaded being poor and alone. I was sick of selling my body and face to strangers. I wondered if I had any usefulness beyond the way I looked and if I would ever truly be able to take care of myself. I couldn't think about my life too much, or the overwhelm would suffocate me.

By the time I was 20 years old, I'd spent two years as a fashion model in New York and Europe. When I first arrived in New York at age 17, walking into each agency was like walking into a church where the religion was pleasure, and the girls were goddesses, immune to the disgrace of ordinary living. Framed photos of supermodels lined the walls, which were decorated in silk and gold. I thought if I could achieve their level of beauty and success, I might be elevated to a height where nothing could harm me, no pain could reach me. It didn't take long for the spell to break and the illusion to crumble.

Sexual advances from middle-aged men were common. Models are supposed to be seen and not heard, so I had to ignore them.

My agent repeatedly told me I was fat, even though I was underweight. Every time I went to her office she wrapped a measuring tape around my waist, hips, and thighs, and declared, "You need to lose fifteen pounds."

Desperate to keep my contract, I asked my model friends for help.

"Lettuce will keep you alive, and only has about fifty calories for a whole head. And cigarettes will curb your appetite," one of them advised.

"Take water pills. You can drop ten pounds in one day if you need to," another added.

"Eat what you want and throw it up. Then you don't have to feel guilty about it afterward," said a third.

I starved myself and took the water pills. When I ate a few slices of pizza at a party, I went into the bathroom and made myself throw up. I compared myself constantly to the other girls, and scrutinized every inch of my body. I felt weak and scared, loaded with a pressure I was too fragile to carry.

Professional modeling was supposed to be the fulfillment of a childhood dream, the culmination of 10 years of beauty pageants, dance lessons, and desperate ambition. But instead of taking me to the Promised Land, it dropped me right back into the dump I had been trying to escape, with a new affinity for vodka, cigarettes, and starvation.

Skinny and heartbroken, I returned to Scranton, Pennsylvania. A whispering of insults inhabited my mind: *Worthless, hopeless, failure, fraud.* Vicious and persistent, they made me want to crawl out of my skin. I masked my fears about myself with big sunglasses and even bigger smiles. I was good at performing, and at giving the impression that everything was *just fine.*

If you didn't know better, Scranton might have seemed quaint with its green mountains, old Victorian houses, and historical railyard. But it was a city stuck in the distant past. Scranton was a coal town with no more coal industry. The ground was empty because all the coal had been extracted for trains in the 1900s. Occasionally, a house fell into a pit, and people would stand around shaking their heads and shrugging their shoulders. There was an exodus of young adults leaving town each June after high school graduation because there were few opportunities for prosperity there. It was what it was. Scranton was a place of catastrophe and abandonment. No one expected anything better.

Madness, like addiction, runs in my family. My mother's father worked in the coal mines after WWII and emerged with drunk fists, which he used on everyone, including her. He died of a heart attack when my mother was 14. Although he was a thug, my mother always talked about him sweetly, as if kicking her down the stairs and holding her brother's hand on the stove were misdemeanors that shouldn't be held against him. Her affection baffled me.

My grandma lived until her 90s. Even on her deathbed, she fondly reminisced about my grandfather, the love of her life.

While my mother's parents embodied German violence and Irish alcoholism, my father's family was the epitome of Italian conceit.

"We are the best," my father told me repeatedly. "You are the best."

Being the best meant I had to have straight As in school, just like my father when he was my age. He learned this perfectionism from his mother, who tore off her clothes in a rage when he made a mistake or got less than 100% in every class.

Luckily, academic intelligence ran in my blood. I made it all the way to a Ph.D. without failing a course. It also helped that I grew up Catholic, which meant a dozen years of formal education in the discipline of "being good." "Good" was brutal competition disguised as sportsmanship, conformity masked as appropriateness, and deception played off as manners, all enforced by the patriarchy. Being forced to be good all the time taught me I was never good enough.

Being back in Scranton after giving up on my childhood dream was a punishing purgatory. I lingered in a place of suffering, waiting for redemption. I didn't have a job. I didn't have any friends. I didn't know what to do. There were no photographers or agents, no measuring tapes or casting calls. The solitude was heavy. The quiet filled with mental chatter. *You're a loser. What's wrong with you? What are you doing with your life?*

I tried to shake it off. I lit a cigarette. I turned on the TV. I needed to find something productive to do.

The only thing I liked half as much as modeling was art. In New York, I went to the Metropolitan Museum of Art on my days off. In each painting, I was transported to another beautiful time and space.

I enrolled in the art program at Keystone College because I couldn't think of anything better to do. Art school in Scranton in 1995 was an angsty teenage drama flick. On the first day of class, I met a boy with a mohawk and baggy shorts who listened to Rage Against the Machine on full volume in his old Highlander. We got high and had sex in his backseat.

I met a few other misfits like Kaitlin, who had a suspicious number of cuts from "shaving," and John, who never showered and only drew pictures of cockroaches. We got tattoos, drank warm beer at backyard parties, and smoked a lot. The combination of nicotine, weed, and alcohol wasn't great for my health, but it made it easy to paint for long hours and it muted the vilifying voice in my mind.

I was hanging out with my motley crew after school one day when I got a call from my brother, Joseph, who is 2 years younger than I.

"Can you come to the hospital? Mom's sick."

I sighed. It was always something with her. Migraines. Herniated discs. Food poisoning. I didn't want to go to the hospital.

The last time I had seen my mom, we had gotten into a stupid fight. I'd stopped by her house, and she was playing terrible folk music in the kitchen. I reached for the dial and turned it off. Normally, she was passive about stuff like that, but not this time.

"What the hell are you doing?" Her face flushed as she walked toward me.

"That music sucks."

"Don't you dare touch my stuff. This is my house. I'll play whatever music I damn well please." She was a few inches shorter than me, but it always felt like she towered over me when she was angry.

She turned the music back on.

It was so rare to see my mother claim any personal space that I didn't even know how to respond. Suddenly, at 52 years old, she had boundaries.

I was still feeling annoyed as I drove to the hospital. My brother had already left for work, so I was going to be stuck with Mom alone.

When I arrived at her room, Mom was writhing in pain. Her face was pale green and she was covered in sweat. She looked really sick.

Suddenly, the argument about folk music seemed absurd.

"Everything will be okay." I brushed the hair out of her eyes.

Mom wore a dazed, terrified expression. "I can't breathe."

"You're breathing just fine."

"Where's the fucking doctor?" I said to the nurse who scurried in and out of the room, adding more narcotics to my mother's IV drip.

"The doctor does rounds at 6," she said matter-of-factly.

"It's 2 in the afternoon!" I cried.

She ignored me.

Time slowed down. The weight of my mother's pain permeated my being. I felt as helpless as she did. Each minute on the clock seemed like an unbearable eternity. Mom faded in and out of consciousness. Her damp hospital gown clung to her skin like Saran wrap. Images flickered on the TV mounted over the bed.

I was not a doctor or a caregiver. I didn't like any of that shit. I liked boys and parties, being pretty and popular. I let other people do the hard things while I avoided as much responsibility as possible. I was not prepared for this. I was ill-equipped to handle my post-adolescent life, let alone an ill parent. This was way beyond my capacity. Someone needed to call an adult to handle it.

Helpless, hopeless, worthless, failure. The menacing inner voice returned with renewed vigor.

I snuck out a few times to smoke in the courtyard. Each time, I returned to the room filled with dread.

Finally, after what seemed like weeks of waiting, the doctor arrived. "Her tests are all negative. I don't know what's wrong with her," he said.

Was this all in her head? I was going to be so pissed if she wasn't actually sick.

"We'll do exploratory surgery to see if we can figure out what's going on," the doctor added.

When Mom conceded to the surgery, I knew things were really bad. She had never been admitted to the hospital before, not even when my father assaulted her. My mother was stubborn. She took her hits like a champ. I had never seen her use a crutch or get a stitch. She was a grin-and-bear-it type of woman who preferred to ride it out at home alone than have anyone fuss over her.

As a very small child, I spent all my time with Mom while Dad studied for his medical school exams or made hospital rounds. Mom's daily work was braiding my hair and pushing me on the swings. Pretty beyond comprehension, my mother was blue-eyed and blonde. She seemed to glow from the inside out. She fluttered, butterfly-like, with gentle movements and kind hands. Sometimes she wore a red satin kimono jacket, a gift from our Japanese neighbor, and my heart beat faster just looking at her.

During the long days of summer, we'd drive down winding country roads to the farms that lay outside town. We stood at the fence and chocolate cows licked my fingers. Mom said I had "moo-cow" eyes, big and brown, rimmed with thick, dark lashes.

Some afternoons, Mom took me on carousel rides at Hershey Park, where she bought me silver-wrapped Kisses, spoiling me with sweetness.

On rainy days, we snuggled up and watched movies about Africa. Mom loved Africa, even though she had never been there. She showed me films about gorillas and safaris, and she said that if she wasn't so afraid of flying, Africa would be the first place she'd go.

Our companionship was effortless and joyful. I knew my mother loved me more than anything in life; she said she loved me so much it felt like her heart was walking around outside her body.

As I sat in the hospital waiting room staring at the ugly orange carpet, there was a faint longing for the tenderness we used to share. In some distant cavern of my heart, I could still feel the lingering love that had filled the first few years of my life.

The exploratory surgery lasted 8 hours. During that time, I explained the situation over and over to Mom's family as they arrived. First, it was her best friend, then her brother and his wife. Finally, her mother, my nana. Mom was a social butterfly, but she was close with only a few. Their responses were panicky and stressful, as I expected. It was one of the many reasons I distanced myself from them.

Each time I told the story, it seemed less and less real, like it was happening to someone else. I felt the onset of a fever.

"You should eat something," my aunt said, handing me some stale plastic-wrapped crackers. I wasn't hungry.

When the doctor finally approached us, he faltered. He couldn't look me in the eye. "Her appendix ruptured. We did the best we could...."

A wave of heat descended on me. My vision blurred. The doctor kept speaking, but I wasn't comprehending the words coming from his mouth. He was like a phantom, hovering in front of me, while I slipped into the throes of a fever dream.

Mom's family freaked out. It was like being surrounded by a swarm of mosquitos. They volleyed a barrage of questions at the doctor.

What next? How long? When can we see her?

The next thing I remember, I was standing in the ICU, where everything was white and sterile and smelled like formaldehyde. Mom lay motionless on a hospital bed. Bags of fluid dripped into her veins. Panels of fluorescent lights flickered overhead. Her skin was transparent and pale. When I spoke to her, she didn't respond. I touched her, but she didn't move.

I felt as if I was falling out of a plane. The weight of disorientation pulled at me like gravity. My veins flooded with adrenaline. My insides twisted into knots. The sight of my mother lying so still was incomprehensible. I couldn't breathe. My vision narrowed to a tunnel, focused exclusively on the fluorescent green pulse of the cardiac monitor...bleep....bleep....bleep....It was the only palpable evidence that my mother was still alive. My mind latched onto that sound and refused to let go.

2

I MUST HAVE LEFT the hospital. I must have driven home. I must have gone to bed, gotten up, gotten dressed, and gone back to the hospital again, but the nightmare of my mother's incarceration in the ICU occupied me so completely that my body moved on automatic pilot.

The surgery had been a failure. They'd waited too long to operate. Her appendix had ruptured hours earlier while she was writhing in pain, and they had ignored it. Instead, they pumped her full of pain meds while she was drowning in poison. She was septic. The infection spread throughout her body. She was in a coma, with a 20% chance of survival. The longer she was unconscious, the more damage there would be when she woke. *If* she survived, she might have brain damage. She might be paralyzed.

I acquired this information in bits and pieces from conversations with doctors and nurses. My mother's best friend worked as a secretary at the hospital, so she was running around collecting medical facts, predictions, and opinions.

A rotation of loved ones filtered in and out for visiting hours. Everyone had the same dumbfounded look on their faces. No one could accept the reality of the situation.

My uncle called my aunt, who was married to a lawyer. They ranted about malpractice and suing the hospital.

My brother and I sat from morning to night in the waiting room. We had the kind of relationship that two refugees have in exile. We were trauma bonded, even before Mom got sick. Although we shared similar circumstances, we did not share similar perspectives.

My relationship with my mother had become combative during my teen years. After my parents' divorce, I lived with my mother and brother. One night when I was about 13 years old, I stood at my bedroom window watching a man escort my mother down the driveway with his hand on the small of her back. It made me sick to my stomach. After writing endless pages of, "I hate you. I hate you. I hate you. I hate you," in my diary, I started to shake. A volcanic wave came up from my gut, into my throat, and lit up my face crimson red. I caught a glimpse of myself in the mirror and something inside said *RUN!*

I climbed out the window and jumped from the roof to the yard. I squatted like an Olympic sprinter and then I ran as hard as I could, down the street past the neighbors and the baseball park. I ran past the old coal mines and streetlamps. I ran until my feeble legs went soft and I landed in the dirt as far away as I had ever been from my house on my own.

Lying in the dirt, alone except for the expansive blue sky, I felt a rush of cleansing breath and the serenity of solitude. For a few precious minutes, I was empty. There was no burning rage. There was no chase and nothing to fight. There was a subtle sense of joy, a palpable taste of relief. This is what it feels like to be free, I thought. I lingered there for a bit, listening to a few chirping birds and the rustling of leaves. Then I felt a cold breeze on my skin. The sun was going down and the warmth of the moment was waning with it. It would be dark soon, and dangerous to be a little girl alone in the world.

I slowly started walking home. My legs grew heavy and little sparks of heat returned to my limbs. My chest tightened and my shoulders collapsed. I tried to make myself as small as possible, wishing I could become completely invisible.

When I crossed the threshold of my house, Mom was waiting for me in the kitchen. Her eyes were daggers, her wrath undeniable. She grabbed me by the hair and dragged me up the stairs. It felt like my scalp was tearing off my head. I didn't resist. There was no point. She sat me in a chair in an empty room. "If you move, you will regret it," she said. I closed my eyes and curled into a fetal position. The deepest pain was not my throbbing head or my solitary confinement. The most cutting pain was knowing we were no longer family. We were enemies.

While I rejected my mother during my teen years, Mom and Joseph grew more and more enmeshed. At the time of her illness, he was 18 and still living at Mom's, and they were closer than ever.

The first thing Joseph did when he went to Mom's bedside was to put the Walkman with his music on her ears. Joseph was obsessed with music, and Mom was obsessed with Joseph. She took him to piano lessons and jazz concerts and bought him a baby grand piano. Joseph recorded songs on cassette tapes and Mom played them relentlessly.

The sun went down and came up again. I relocated from my apartment into my childhood house so Joseph and I could travel back and forth to the hospital together. I despised that house. The wallpaper smelled like nicotine and regret. The furniture was covered with dust and disgust. Almost everything bad that had ever happened to me had happened in that house. I felt a rage in my gut just walking up and down the creaking stairs. It was 14 rooms too big, all of them stuffed with junk. Every drawer, cabinet, and closet overflowed with useless things Mom had collected.

Joseph thought the place was charming. The stained-glass windows, the 3rd-floor tower, the nooks and crannies where the cats liked to nap. He never had a bad thing to say about the house, or about anything, for that matter. Where he was yin, I was yang. Where I was darkness, he was light. His sensitivity was something precious I tried to protect for a long time but eventually came to resent.

At first, there weren't many decisions to be made about Mom's care. I held her hands and covered her with a blue blanket. If my mother was still inside her limp body, I couldn't tell. She looked as hollow as a fish washed up on shore. The sensation of the fever dream persisted, a constant disorientation. I heard the persistent tone of the monitor in my mind...bleep....bleep....bleep....even when I wasn't standing next to it.

After a week or so, Mom's toes curled into a fist. It's called "foot drop," a common symptom when you're bedridden. It was gruesome to look at, like the feet of the Wicked Witch under the house in *The Wizard of Oz*.

I bought Mom sneakers to keep her feet upright. It wasn't a gesture of hopefulness; it was an act of utility. I thought to myself at the counter, she's never going to walk in these. I wouldn't dare say that to Joseph or my grandma or anyone else who was holding a daily vigil of optimism. I was expecting the worst. Things never work out for me, I thought, why would this be any different?

My feverish symptoms increased as my mother's condition declined. I had sweats and chills. Shivers. I grew weak.

Mom's lungs filled with fluid. Bacteria colonized her airways, and she got nosocomial pneumonia. It was maybe the 14th day when they told us that she was unable to breathe on her own without support from a ventilator.

There were no windows in the ICU, and no way to know if it was night or day. It was dark when we arrived and dark when we left, insidious darkness that grew in proportion to Mom's illness and my terror.

The tectonic plates of the earth were shifting. Mom was leaving, slowly but surely. I was the next in succession.

Worthless, hopeless, failure, fraud.

There was no way I could take care of myself without a parent to fall back on.

Who was going to be the adult? Who was going to be the responsible one? Who was going to tell me how much I was screwing up my life and how I needed to do better?

It had been years since I had spoken to my father. He never came to the hospital, even though he knew what was happening. Dad never attended a beauty pageant, dance recital, school conference, or birthday party. He existed in a separate universe, where people revolved around him, not the other way around.

When they put Mom on the ventilator, Joseph and I started to bicker.

"She didn't want this. She told us she never wanted to be on life support," I said.

"She's going to wake up. It's going to be fine," Joseph insisted.

"It's not going to be fine.," I snapped. "Even if she woke up now, she would be so fucked up we'd have to take care of her for the rest of her life."

"Then we'll take care of her." Joseph's eyes blazed with determination.

I saw my life flash before my eyes—a future of living in Mom's house, being her private nurse, and waiting years for her to die. It was a fate worse than death, for both of us.

"I don't want to take care of her," I told my brother.

His jaw tightened. "Then I'll take care of her."

I shook my head. "This is ridiculous."

I was impudent and selfish, with no regard for what Joseph wanted. I felt no obligation to make him or anyone else happy. The waiting was wearing me down, draining my patience, eroding my good girl façade.

15 days went by. Then 20. Then 25. Time collapsed, past-present-future merging into a weightless limbo. The phone rang, or a door slammed, and I'd jump like a feral cat.

I was consumed with thoughts of my mother. I could think of nothing else. Fights with her played over and over, scenes of us hurling slurs at each other. Each memory stung with a heartbreaking venom.

I had flashbacks from when I was nine. My parents were in the middle of divorcing when I became ill. I felt a burning sensation when I peed, but I didn't want Mom and Dad to know. I was afraid that I had done something wrong, that I was somehow to blame for the pain. I stopped eating and drinking. My tongue stuck to the roof of my mouth. My lips cracked. Then I lost track of where my body ended and where the world began.

Mom noticed my deterioration and took me to the emergency room. "Your temperature is 105! You could have died!" She exclaimed as they admitted me for a kidney infection.

Mom held my hand while masked people stuck catheters in my private parts. I lay on a metal table, legs spread wide. The weighted radiation shield felt like a sandbag on my chest. A lady told me to pee on the table while she operated a camera that looked like a giant alien hovering over me as it took black and white pictures of my insides. I faded in and out of consciousness. Tubes invaded my arm. A glossy bag of fluid filled me up like a water balloon. There was pain. So much dizzying pain that had nowhere to go.

Mom was there the whole time, stoic and calm, never complaining or impatient. Sometimes I felt her worry or caught a glimpse of her trembling hand. But mostly, she was steady and respectful.

Why couldn't I be like that for her now? I was failing her. I was failing myself.

On the 29th day, the doctor said, "She no longer has any brain functions. She will not regain consciousness. Do you want to turn off the ventilator?"

Time stopped. The fever burned brighter within me. I was suspended in a state of slow motion falling toward the ground. I was tumbling, tumbling, tumbling, and yet standing perfectly still. I knew he was waiting for me to respond, but the gravitational pull was so strong even words could not escape. I might have nodded. I might have answered. But I was so far from my body, anything could have happened.

On the 30th day, I gathered with my brother, uncle, aunt, and grandmother around Mom's bed. The staff turned off the machines. It was unceremonial. I didn't speak. I didn't cry. I didn't even flinch when the nurse turned to me and said, "Where do you want to have the funeral?"

Church was one of the most important places of my childhood. Mom never let us miss a Sunday service or opt out of any sacrament, especially confession. She carried rosary beads in her purse and had images of saints scattered throughout the house. She prayed to St. Anthony when we lost something. She prayed to Mother Mary for healing. There was a crucifix over the kitchen door and a nativity scene under the Christmas tree.

My mother's version of church was less about celebration and resurrection, and more about penance and shame. One time, I heard the priest yelling at her in the confessional booth. Then she came out to the pew, got on her knees, and prayed like her life depended on it.

When I was six years old, Mom enrolled me in Catholic school. She wrapped me in a blue plaid skirt and dropped me off at a white brick building a few blocks from home. Men and women dressed in black floated through the hallways. A dying man hung on a cross in every room. Next door to my school was a tall stone church with colored glass windows and a hundred rows of pews where we knelt and sang and prayed.

In that building, I was introduced to God for the first time. Men in robes swung incense from a canister on a long noisy chain. They chanted mysteries in Latin and English and turned bread into "The Flesh of Our Savior."

On the day of my First Holy Communion when I was seven years old, I walked down the long aisle in a frilly white dress. On either side of me, tall white columns loomed bigger than the trees. I felt far away from everything, especially my family. I walked quietly and orderly like we were taught in rehearsal, stepping carefully because I didn't want to make a mistake. The space was so big, so thick with chanting and prayer. The music was mesmerizing, and I felt a bit lightheaded. The closer I got to the man at the altar, the more I felt like a spell was being cast.

My right hand cupped beneath my left just like we'd practiced countless times. I raised my palms. The priest held a circle of bread in front of me. We locked eyes and he said, "Body of Christ."

Everything seemed to drop away as the bread slowly descended into my hands. I took the host and put it in my mouth. As I walked back to the pew, I felt the bread on my tongue. As it disintegrated, I felt some intangible faith being passed on to me.

When we entered the church for my mother's funeral, I didn't know what my faith was. I no longer had a relationship with God. It had been a dozen years since my First Holy Communion, and my beliefs had shifted from, *God is my protector,* to *God has abandoned me just like everyone else in my life.* I no longer prayed for anything. I didn't go to church. I didn't take the sacraments. I was convinced that religion was for people who were too lazy to think for themselves, or too brainwashed to see through all the patriarchal bullshit.

My brother hunched over his keyboard alongside the altar at the end of the long aisle. His hands moved back and forth over the keys.

He was so broken. As he sang a chilling tribute that he had written for my mother, it seemed as if his insides were spilling out with the musical notes onto the floor.

There were a dozen or so people in the pews. And a lot of crying; the kind of crying people do when there's an injustice, not just a loss. The kind of crying at crime scenes, and car accidents, and when a baby drowns in a pool.

I was not crying. I was stunned. The fever that had been building for weeks, the dreams that accompanied night sweats and shortness of breath, the long waking nightmare that had been my life for a month, shifted into hallucination.

As I approached the casket where my mother lay dressed in a respectable pink dress and gold earrings, I heard her say, "I'm not in there. I'm over here." I turned quickly to the area behind the casket. Mom's being, a transparent shimmering, was as real as the agonizing music and the perfumed scent of the altar candles. In my mind, she reassured me that everything was fine.

"I'm ok," she said. "I'm actually better than ok. I feel so much peace. I feel free."

A wave of joy washed over me. I could feel that what Mom was saying was true. I could feel what she was feeling. It was as if we were no longer separate, but one and the same.

I looked around. The music was still playing. People were still crying. *Am I the only one who can hear her?*

I looked back at her body in the casket. It was like a large porcelain doll version of my mother. I raised my eyes to the misty area behind the casket. I could feel my mom smirking at me.

"Don't worry," she said, "you're not crazy."

A combination of fear and relief, confusion and clarity, elation and panic rose in me. Followed by more waves of joy.

"Tell them I'm ok," Mom said. "Tell them not to worry."

I made my way to the podium for the eulogy. I stared out at the crowd. The church was so big, the doors at the far back were like headlights at the end of a dark tunnel. As if I was under a spell, I felt everything drop away. It was just like being back at my First Holy Communion, with the mesmerizing energy of some intangible spiritual energy.

I chose my words carefully. "Um, Mom is doing fine... I mean, Mom is in a better place. We should be happy that she's at peace, that she is no longer suffering." Words seemed absurd. I felt so far away from everyone except my mother. As supernatural as it was, my connection to Mom was clear and distinct. It was a direct experience of something, dare I say, *divine.*

We moved from the church to the cemetery. There must have been a procession, but I don't recall. I remember sitting graveside on a black folding chair, surrounded by headstones. I recall the warmth of the sun on my face. My mom's best friend read a poem, and everyone bawled.

I thought that being outside might bring a fresh perspective, might dissipate the weird energy and bring me back to Earth.

I was wrong.

I stared at the grave as they lowered Mom's casket into the ground. I turned to look at the bush next to me. There was a caterpillar on a leaf. Through the eyes of the insect, I felt Mom looking at me.

I thought I was losing my mind.

Then Mom left the caterpillar like a wisp of smoke and swirled around the trees, the sky, the clouds, all the while telling me that the universe is made of energy, she is made of energy, everything is energy, and she is part of everything. Physical reality dropped away. I perceived the world as a multi-dimensional prism of light. I could no longer see the casket or the grave, the priest or the crying mourners, the head-stones or the folding chairs. I was lost in some psychedelic trip, the likes of which would make Timothy Leary's head spin.

It was fucking weird.

I had no context for the experience. Nothing in modern medicine or my dozen years of Catholic school validated this. Nothing in the Bible could back it up. *Who would believe me?* Everyone would think I was on drugs, but I had never taken a hard drug in my life.

How could my brain manufacture this? Was it the stress? The lack of sleep? What's the purpose of this?

I felt like Mom was trying to tell me something really important, but I had no way to decode it. No way to understand the cryptic message, or comprehend the significance of the experience.

It would be many years and many spiritual experiences later before I understood the impact of that profound moment. It would take a lifetime before I could grasp that on the day of her death my mother showed me, a floundering twenty-one-year-old with little ambition and no direction, the purpose of my life.

3

THERE IS SOMETHING ABOUT the death of a parent, especially your mother, that brings the finite quality of life into sharp focus. Before Mom's death, I had the unreal sense there was plenty of time to flounder because life goes on forever, or at least until some very distant date in the future. Waking up on the day after her funeral, not only did I recognize life had an end, it was a hell of a lot closer than I had realized.

How much time do I have left? What am I supposed to be doing? These questions burned in me. Mom always said her two greatest accomplishments were my brother and me. I didn't want a husband or children. What, if anything, would be my achievements when I arrived at the finish line of my life?

The existential pressure of my life purpose, mixed with the mind-bending mirage at mom's funeral, created a vice on my head like a migraine. Shame and anxiety woke me repeatedly during the night. I wobbled through my days, desperately seeking numbing relief from any substance or distraction, which led to more fights with my brother and more isolation from everyone.

For a year or so before she died, Mom had been nagging me to go to a psychiatrist. She said I was self-destructive and out of control. I thought she was full of shit. If anyone needed therapy it was her, not me.

Writhing in constant discomfort, unable to purge memories of the ICU from my mind, I needed something stronger than alcohol and cigarettes to help me forget. I pulled out the piece of paper with the name and number of the doctor Mom had given me. I agonized over whether or not to call. I really wanted drugs. Prozac. Xanax. Klonopin. Anything. But I hated physicians. Doctors—psychiatrists like my father, especially—were lunatics, or useless like the morons who hadn't helped my mother.

I couldn't decide which was worse: visiting a doctor or living with chronic excruciating pain, which was both psychic and physical. An internal struggle twisted my guts in knots for weeks until I finally broke down and made an appointment.

Dr. Kelly opened the door to her office and motioned for me to come in. I was wearing my art-student uniform, dirty overalls and Converse sneakers. I had a shaved head and fresh armband tattoo on display. In stark contrast, Dr. Kelly was dressed like a librarian, with a perfect blond bob that swished on her shoulders when she walked. I plopped down, stiff and guarded, on the leather couch she indicated.

If she asks me to lie down, I'm outta here, I thought.

"What brings you here today?" Dr. Kelly said.

My head was spinning with the things I could never tell her: I was scared all the time. I had no idea what I was doing with my life. I felt shattered and confused and breathless. If, God forbid, I accidentally told Dr. Kelly I could talk to the ghost of my dead mother, I was sure she would lock me up and throw away the key.

"I, um, don't feel good," I said.

Admitting to a total stranger that I didn't feel well took a monumental effort. I worried she might judge me or punish me. I hadn't ever told my parents when I didn't feel good, even when I had that kidney infection. *If you don't speak it, it isn't happening,* was an unspoken covenant in my family.

"Can you be more specific?" Dr. Kelly seemed genuinely concerned, which unnerved me.

"I have nightmares and panic attacks. I feel like shit most of the time," I managed to get out in a low voice.

"Oh, I'm so sorry to hear that. Do you know what's causing this?" She had a personalized pen poised in her hand, ready to take notes.

I sat there motionless. I wanted a prescription, not a conversation.

"You might feel better if you talk about it," she said gently.

I picked at my cuticles until they bled as I tried to come up with something to say. I needed to tell her something without revealing anything. If I didn't get the meds I came for, the trip would be pointless.

I decided to stick to the bare facts. "My mother died."

"I'm sorry for your loss," she said. "That must be really tough." Her eyes held warmth and compassion as if she truly was sorry about it.

"Uh-huh," I muttered, avoiding eye contact. The grief beneath my composure threatened to bubble to the surface and betray me. I stiffened every fiber of my being to prevent tears from coming. *How long did I have to endure this?* A clock with gold hands mocked me with its slow-motion movement.

"I can give you something to calm your nervous system, but I'd like you to come back once a week so we can monitor your progress," Dr. Kelly said. "It will take several weeks before you begin to benefit from treatment."

"Ok," I said, my eyes fixed on drops of paint on my pants. I was clenching my jaw and grinding my teeth. I'd agree to anything as long as I walked out of her suffocating office with a script in my hand.

When she handed me the small sheet of paper with *Paxil 20mg* scribbled on it, I felt relieved. I briefly looked up at Dr. Kelly. She gave me a soft, genuine smile. I felt a spark in my heart like she had touched an unguarded part of me. I quickly looked away. It was not safe to be close to her. It wasn't safe to be close to anyone.

I reluctantly returned to Dr. Kelly the following week. I was light-headed, with a sensation of pins and needles all over my body. I felt the mild effects of the antidepressants, but they barely curbed the insomnia or overwhelm that plagued me. They definitely didn't penetrate the frozen layers of trauma or the countless unspeakable memories living and pulsating inside of me.

"How are you feeling?" Dr. Kelly studied me through her dainty glasses.

Here we go again, I thought. I wanted drugs, and she wanted to help me.

"Not so good."

"Well, it can take up to 6 weeks to improve," she said. "Are you sleeping ok?"

"Nope."

"How about your appetite? Are you eating?"

"Nope.'"

"Concentration? Focus?"

"Not good."

She took a deep breath and let out a sigh. "Well, I can give you something for sleep and another medication for anxiety. Hopefully, that will help."

Yeah, let's hope, I thought.

"I'd like to learn more about you," she said. I could feel her concern radiating in my direction, which made me squirm on the couch. I wrapped my legs around each other until I was twisted into a pretzel from the waist down.

Since she was giving me more meds, I felt like I had to give her something in return. "Like what?" I said.

"Tell me about your family. Do you have brothers or sisters?"

I'm sure this was a standard question for a new patient, but for me, it was Pandora's box of family drama. My father had married three times. My mother was his first wife. They had me and my brother Joseph. My father had 2 children with his second wife, whom he also divorced. Then he married again and had 3 more children.

The sibling who mattered most to me was Joseph. I fell in love with him when he was a chubby 2-year-old and I was 5. Joseph had a golden head of hair like Mom and tiny teeth that sparkled when he smiled. He was smart and funny and did anything I told him to do. When Mom and Dad slept late on the weekends, we made forts out of sheets and disappeared into a world of make-believe captives. We piled the couch pillows high into a crooked tower and leaped off them onto a foam mattress. My brother had a big laugh. His entire body shook as he flew through the air and bounced up and down on the cushions.

In 1982, about a year before my parents' divorce, Mom and Dad planned a vacation for us, a getaway to have some family fun. I was eight, Joseph not quite six. The four of us road-tripped to upstate New York to see the legendary Niagara Falls. We packed the 1970 Opel GT with snacks and 8-track tapes and headed a couple of hours north to the Canadian border. Joseph and I were squeezed onto the shelf in the back window. Mom and Dad seemed playful and excited. I let myself enjoy the passing of trees and disco music. On good days like that one, it seemed like maybe everything was going to be ok.

It was close to sunset when we arrived and stood at the observation tower, three-hundred-feet above the cliff waters. Dad smiled mischievously as he wrapped his arms around Joseph's waist and lifted him off the ground. A flash of fear filled Mom's eyes. Just as quickly as it had come, she hid it. Her body stiffened.

I looked back and forth between Mom and Dad as Dad held Joseph over the guard railing. He laughed maniacally like a villain. Mom shook with fear. My brother cried so hard it looked like his eyes were bleeding. Rage blazed inside me. It consumed my entire being.

For five years I'd been watching episodes like this in absolute helplessness. My whole life I tried to be good, following the rules, worrying that if I stepped out of line, my father would hit me like he sometimes hit my mother. Dad repeatedly called me his "Little Princess," but who knew what he would do if I stopped playing the part. He was no longer a parent to me; he was a threat. As I watched him torture my brother, the smoldering anger inside me erupted into a wildfire. In a flash, I realized I would do anything to protect my brother. If I had to, I would even kill my father.

I didn't tell Dr. Kelly about my unbridled anger or my homicidal thoughts at Niagara Falls. Instead, I told her I had a brother who played piano, and that we used to get along pretty well but now it seemed like we were growing apart.

Dr. Kelly was sympathetic but not patronizing. She was persistent but not impatient. She radiated kindness and confidence. She revealed nothing about herself but she appeared happy and healthy and self-sufficient. She challenged my assumptions. She was a doctor, but not a corrupt one. After a few appointments, I was amazed and shocked at how much I admired her. She was the first person I had ever met who seemed to actually have her shit together.

More than a cocktail of medications I needed a mentor, but I didn't know what a mentor was. It felt like there were so many things I was supposed to be doing—going to college, getting top grades, becoming significant and successful, yet I couldn't even figure out how to take care of myself.

Being human is complicated, and no one gives you instructions on how to do it. No one teaches you how to take care of an ever-changing body, unruly emotions, a lawless mind, and a wild spirit. Perhaps in healthy families, parents play this role. Maybe teachers step in sometimes to fill the gap.

From as early as I can remember, there were too many big things coming at me, and I had no idea how to handle them. I didn't have a guide for navigating life—decoding the signs that would help me meet my basic needs and lead me to a sense of well-being. Phrases like "self-care" and "self-love" didn't exist in conversation in the 1990s. It would be years before I would understand the connections between my mind and body, and how my habits were truly affecting me. I was way behind the curve, or at least it felt that way.

Everyone deserves a guide through the perilous years of young adulthood. Honestly, we need role models at every age, people to look up to who align with our values. But I couldn't discover my values when I was so busy trying to please everyone around me. I compared myself constantly to others and relied on external validation for my self-esteem and self-worth. The media told me I had to be pretty and perfect, which was becoming more and more difficult. I needed someone to tell me what to do, or at least give me a hint. Maybe Dr. Kelly can give me some advice, I thought. I lowered my guard slightly and let her in.

Little by little, week after week, I shared my life with her. It was much easier to talk about the present than the past. I told her about my friends and art classes. I didn't know if I wanted to be an artist, but I couldn't think of anything else to do. We discussed modeling, and how my agent regularly wrapped me in a measuring tape and told me I needed to lose 15 lbs. Dr. Kelly reassured me I wasn't fat, even though I was still convinced I needed to shed some weight.

Now and then, Dr. Kelly steered the conversation toward my parents and I froze as if an oncoming train was about to hit me. Time and space collapsed. I was a small child again, sitting in the dark, waiting for the police to arrive. In those moments, I knew I had to change the topic quickly or get as far away from Dr. Kelly as possible. Once a traumatic memory took full hold of me, I might be flooded with panic as I tumbled, lost in some nightmare from my childhood, over and over. It could take hours to right my mind and come back to present-time reality. I was convinced that feeling so much intensity made me weak and pathetic. And I was certain that if I felt my feelings completely, I would shatter into pieces.

Dr. Kelly sensed my alarm and backed off, giving me room to breathe. Sometimes, I managed to say a few words, just enough to hint at the bigger picture. Sometimes I felt mute. I just couldn't get any words out. Dr. Kelly waited until the emotion settled before she continued the conversation. She was savvy enough to know that I was doing my best and optimistic enough to believe that I would find my words in time.

My relationship with Dr. Kelly was the antithesis of my relationship with my parents. Dr. Kelly created safe space. Not once in the four years I visited her did I have to run out of the room for fear of being pushed beyond my boundaries. I never raised my voice at her or wished her ill will. We shared mutual respect and acceptance. Dr. Kelly let me be exactly who I was without having to change anything, which eventually inspired me to change everything.

Two years into my treatment with Dr. Kelly, I finished my art courses. I needed to commit to a career in art or find a new direction. Dr. Kelly's curiosity about me piqued my interest in myself. The more questions Dr. Kelly asked, the stronger my need to understand the things that had happened to me. Why did I freak out at the thought of my past? Why was I acting the way I did? Was I destined to be crazy, or could I become a functional adult?

There was no internet in 1996. No smartphones. No Google searches. When I wanted to understand something, I had to pick up a book and read about it. A few books were massively popular at the time. *Men are From Mars, Women are From Venus* proposed that men and women came from different planets, which reinforced my belief in the hopelessness of romantic relationships.

Another book, *The Celestine Prophecy*, described fictional mystical experiences that were uncanny in their similarity to my own, which both validated and terrified me.

The third book, *Prozac Nation*, was a rollercoaster ride of mental illness, suicide, and medication—topics that hit too close to home. The author, Elizabeth Wurtzel, was much braver than I in her naked confessions. I did not have the courage she had to bare my soul to one person, let alone the whole world.

I read all of these books, and a dozen more I found at the local bookstore. It was a personal scavenger hunt I pursued with pride. I shared my thoughts with Dr. Kelly in our weekly sessions. She encouraged me to keep reading and keep learning. She guided me toward assessments and personality tests to explore. Each one gave me clues about myself, which I assembled like pieces of a puzzle. Thanks to the Myers-Briggs test, I discovered I was naturally extroverted, intuitive, empathic, and organized. The Enneagram revealed I valued achievements above all else. My emotional intelligence score registered about 2 out of 10, which explained why I could rarely find the words to adequately express what was happening inside me.

With each conversation, Dr. Kelly encouraged and supported me. She saw something in me that I couldn't see in myself—some pure goodness buried under the ashes. She spoke to that part of me when we were together, telling me I was smart and special, strong and brave.

One day, out of the blue, she said, "I think you should get a degree in psychology. You have a natural talent for understanding the mind."

Her words jolted me. I'd never thought of being a psychologist. "Really? Me?"

She recommended I apply to a college about an hour away. I'd be close enough to stay in therapy but far enough to feel some relief from

Scranton. Her suggestion lifted my spirit in a way I hadn't felt in a long time. It appealed because it was a "real" career. It was aspirational and challenging, noble and intellectual. Something about Dr. Kelly's confidence in me made me confident in myself. I filled out an application. When I was accepted, I enrolled at East Stroudsburg University.

4

A FEW MONTHS LATER, I moved into a dorm room on the ESU campus. I was a swirling mixture of joy and pain, ease and panic. The campus was surrounded by trees, rivers, hiking trails, and one quaint street with a few dive bars and antique shops. About two thousand kids from surrounding towns self-segregated into cliques—jocks, nerds, Greeks, and theatre geeks. I unwrapped twin-size bedsheets and put them on the plastic mattress of the small metal bed. I hung a poster of a Georgia O'Keefe painting on the wall above my desk.

I was staring out the dusty window overlooking the lawn when a black crow landed on a branch and cawed in my direction. She gave me the same feeling as the caterpillar on the day of my mother's funeral. There was no mystical spectacle this time, just a sense that Mom was watching me and trying to communicate. It was loud but whispering. I believed it and doubted it simultaneously.

It was not the first time I had seen the crow. She appeared now and then, and afterward, I got new ideas or messages. She was laying down clues like breadcrumbs for me to follow. She was guiding me toward something. *But what?*

Mom's presence made me feel both crazier and saner. The world was new and different. Or maybe *I* was new and different. Regardless, I wanted things to make sense. I wanted to know my purpose; what I was here to be and do.

I traveled down academic hallways of white-buffed floors and bulletin boards to Abnormal Psych, Statistics, and Personality Theory classes. I listened to professors give lectures on Freudian philosophies and quantitative reality. I read about scientific experiments and clinical trials. My textbooks revealed a world where everything could be orderly, organized, and explained. It was a relief. I found safety in thinking that others had all the answers.

But the psychology textbooks didn't explain my psychedelic trip or communicating with my mother, so I sought out stories from the mystical traditions of ancient Tibetans and Native Americans. I discovered that there were many people in history, especially in indigenous cultures, who communicated with the dead. I learned the crow symbolized death and mystery, guiding human souls to the afterlife.

I struggled to accept my supernatural experiences. I wanted to shake off the mystical mysteries of Mom's death—or at least keep them at a safe distance. I wanted a degree and a career, money and a boyfriend. I wanted upward mobility, emotional stability, and personal security. I wanted the normalcy that was winning at the game of life and living happily ever after.

Studying the habits of the people around me proved just as revealing as my assigned courses. The boys gathered in packs in the cafeteria, reveling in stories of binge drinking and sexual conquests. The girls tore out magazine pictures of impossibly thin models and hung them on their walls. Hazing lurked in the dark, and posturing stood tall in the light. We were all learning what it meant to be men and women:

acceptable, lovable, and safe, in a culture that still smelled like the 1950s to me. I badly wanted to have faith in normalcy. I wanted all of it to be real.

I took on jobs as a resident advisor and orientation leader, moving up the ladder as an ambassador for the "warrior" way of life, as they called it. I did rounds in the halls and led campus tours. I starred in the welcome video projected at the opening assembly. By all accounts, I was mastering the game and becoming a role model others could look up to.

But I also had a nagging feeling that I had a calling, something more significant than the false directions I had received for the first twenty years of my life. Something more meaningful than the characters and roles I'd been instructed to play. This sense of calling felt unfamiliar but unthreatening. I felt like an intangible mystery was speaking to me. Common things like leaves and trees were dazzling with personality. A spider in her crystal web seemed magical and brilliant. I didn't have words for it, but sometimes it felt more real than physical reality.

Across campus sat the fine arts building—a spacious theatre and dance studio where I found a different kind of rhythm. Dropping down into my legs, I rediscovered the movement that had carried me through many days as a dancing kid. I joined the dance company and practiced for a performance of *Jesus Christ Superstar*—a collaboration with the theatre crowd.

On the first day of rehearsal, I met Chris. He was all the things I loved to hate about a guy—popular and smug, a jock and a frat boy. He could sing, dance, and make everyone laugh when he told raunchy jokes. In high school, he was a football star, baseball star, and lead actor in the plays. He even had a pretty blond cheerleader girlfriend. He had six-pack abs, baby blue eyes, and dirty blond hair. I was determined to dislike him.

"I saw you the first day you were here," he said.

"You did?"

"Yeah, you were walking around by yourself."

"You didn't say anything to me."

"I didn't know you, so I didn't say anything, but I noticed you immediately. You stand out from other girls."

I tried to hide how much I liked the compliment.

A subtle hunger awakened in me after our encounter. He was the guy that a normal girl would get, and I was anything but that. But he'd noticed me. What did that mean? Maybe I wanted to be wanted, or maybe he was a better charmer than I expected. Whatever it was, I couldn't get him out of my head.

On one of my evening walks around the dorm, I passed by an open door and heard singing drifting into the hall.

"It must have been love, but it's over now; it must have been good, but I lost it somehow." It was a male voice, tender and sweet, the kind of voice that makes you turn up the volume on the radio.

I stopped and listened. I felt a rush of openness in my heart. I wanted to lean into the voice, to fall into it and dissolve in the beauty of the sound.

I stuck my head inside the dark room and said, "Hello?"

"Hey," a voice said.

Then I saw his face. "Chris?"

Oh my god. He's singing a love song. Who is this guy?

"Oh, hey, Gabrielle. What's up?"

"Is that you singing?"

"Yeah."

Enchanted, I could sense he had a hunger that matched my own. We flirted, and when I got back to my room, there was a lightness of being, like the weight of unbearable responsibility I had been carrying was replaced by joy. This euphoria lasted for several months as I was free-falling into love for the first time.

Just as I was feeling content and happy, my brother called. "Will you come and meet Dad with me?" he asked.

Everything in my body screamed NO. I didn't want to be in the same room with my father any more than I wanted to climb into a cage with a shark.

"Why?" I asked.

Dad lived with his third wife and their three children on one hundred acres of land, in a mansion with an indoor pool and six-car garage. I'd never been there, and I barely knew Dad's wife or the boys.

I didn't know if Dad knew I had graduated from high school or moved to New York for modeling. He hadn't come to Mom's funeral. He didn't even send a card.

"He called me," my brother said. "He wants to see us."

"I don't want to see him."

"Please. I want us to be a family."

Even though he was 20 years old, Joseph was still my baby brother. My buddy for playing records and pinball games and hide-and-seek. I wanted to please him, protect him. I wanted to be the big sister he needed me to be.

"What do you want me to do?" I asked.

"Just meet with him. Give it a chance."

Joseph and I walked into a therapist's office. I was not happy to be there. As soon as I saw my father, I was six years old again. My whole being was clenched with tension, and it was difficult to breathe. I sat on a hard chair next to the therapist, as far away from Dad as possible. He sat on the couch next to my brother.

"Your dad would like to make amends to you," the therapist explained. "He would like to have a relationship with you."

The woman looked at my father. "Isn't that right?"

Dad nodded. He turned to me. "Why are you so cold? Why do you look at me like that?"

Shock mixed with grief, rage, and fear inside me. I felt as if I was freefalling out of a skyscraper.

The therapist said, "I think what your dad wants to know is, what are you thinking? What are you feeling?"

Memories exploded in me like fireworks, bright and hot.

"I remember. He thinks I don't, but I do." I couldn't believe the words coming out of my mouth. My brother looked angry that I was being difficult.

The therapist frowned. "What do you remember?"

Just be quiet. Bite your tongue, for God's sake, some part of me urged.

Instead, I heard myself say, "I remember that he was a monster." I trembled all over. My gut burned. I felt nauseous. *Why was I saying this out loud?*

The therapist looked baffled. She turned to my father. "Is that true?"

My father's gaze dropped to the floor. "I don't remember everything," he mumbled. "I know it was bad, but I don't remember it all."

I closed my eyes and clenched my fists. Rage threatened to erupt, and I feared I would vomit right there on the therapist's beige carpeting.

She addressed my brother. "Do you remember?"

He shook his head.

My rage and anxiety flared even brighter. *How could he not remember? Is he choosing to forget?*

The therapist coughed. She adjusted herself in her chair. I sensed that she didn't know what to do or say. The air was hot and sticky. Dad's after-shave permeated the room.

After a few seconds, the therapist regained her composure. "Would you like to have a relationship with your father?" she asked my brother.

"Yes." His answer was immediate and unequivocal. With it, the threads of our bond unraveled, a thousand woven fibers fraying at the seams.

He wants to be part of Daddy's tribe. The tribe of lies, deceit, abuse, and control. Mom is gone. Am I really going to lose Joseph, too?

The therapist turned to me. "Would you like to have a relationship with your father?"

The weight of all the love, sympathy, and devotion I had for my brother felt so heavy on my chest that I struggled to catch my breath. I'd do anything for Joseph. Anything but this. I could not, would not, join my father's tribe for him. "I don't think so," I said.

The loss of the one family member I remained close to tore through me so sharply that I gasped. The room split in two. I stared at the three of them in their pack on the other side of an invisible chasm far wider than the few feet separating us in the therapist's office. My body tingled and my legs grew weak. I feared that if I stood, they'd give out instead of holding me up. I felt myself suspended between who I once was and who I was becoming.

"You should forgive him," my brother pleaded. "I really want you to forgive him." Joseph had hunched shoulders and dark circles under his eyes. He looked like he had been crying for months. Mom's death had blown a hole through the middle of him. I felt the seduction of his suffering, the ache to be with him. But it wasn't enough to change my mind.

"You don't hate me as much as you think you do," Dad said. He looked older. Silver ran through his thick black hair. I hated his arrogance, the way he assumed he knew me better than I knew myself. Yet he was right. I wanted to be his little girl again, the child he'd carried up to the podium and across the stage at his medical school graduation. I felt the seduction of loyalty and compassion and the pleasure he vibrated when he held me. I wanted to hug him and say, "It's okay, Daddy. Everything will be ok. I love you." But I couldn't do it. I couldn't live in his dark world again. I would not sacrifice myself for him.

"I'm sorry. I have to go." I stood up from the chair, and thankfully my legs cooperated. A cascade of tears fell from my eyes as I walked out of the room and closed the door.

After the showdown in the therapist's office, it was a relief to have Chris distract me. Chemistry grew between us as we prepared for the opening night of *Jesus Christ Superstar*. When he wrapped my feet in Ace bandages to soothe my aching shin splints, I nearly pounced on him with lust.

The curtain finally opened, and I leaped onto the stage with a rush of adrenaline and emotion, like I was launching into a fairy tale. I spun and swirled with the other dancers to the chorus songs while hundreds of excited faces beamed at us.

Chris sang with that divinity that made me dizzy. With each scene, the momentum grew. When it was time for our solo I glided toward him, arm outstretched, and reached for his hand. He was supposed to reach back toward me empty-handed but instead, he was holding a rose. We locked eyes. I lost my breath. The hunger completely devoured me.

When the curtain closed, we giggled and buzzed all the way to the afterparty. Inside the house, the soundtrack from the show was playing. We sang along. We clapped our hands. I didn't think the night could be any better. I had never been more electric or alive.

Chris leaned in and kissed me. I closed my eyes. Everything was white, like snow, but warm, like summer. My whole body melted. I couldn't feel where he stopped and I began.

Chris and I became inseparable. When I wasn't with him, I dreamt about being together. Chris made me feel loved and worthy, two things I'd yearned for all my life. He was more than the pretty boy I'd thought he was when we first met. He had scars, just like me, from his angry father and his cheating girlfriend. When he told me about the time his dad forced him to eat by shoving food in his mouth, I felt his pain as my own. When I told him my stories, his eyes welled with tears. We bonded over our pain as much as we did our pleasure.

Above all else, Chris was passionate about family. He pitched the idea of getting married and starting a family to me almost immediately. We would move back to his small Pennsylvania town. He had a good job in a warehouse and was expecting a promotion. I could find work, and we could settle down. It would be a perfect life.

Everything in my body said YES to Chris, but everything in my mind said NO to marriage and children. My sense of higher purpose was growing stronger every day. I had connected with many girls on campus, inside and outside the classroom. I presented research about body image, eating disorders, and beauty myths in my psychology classes. I shared my experience of the modeling industry and showed pictures of anorexic women that bore an uncanny resemblance to the teen models I knew. Girls came up to me afterward and confessed secrets of bulimia and rape. I was astonished. I had no idea how many women were being affected by physical and psychological violence. It enraged and inspired me to do more. I created a monthly meeting in our dorm. A small but loyal following gathered, relieved to have a safe space to share.

In one meeting, a freshman girl was moved to tears. She shared her struggle and despair. "Can you help me?" she asked. I was speechless. I didn't know how to help her, but I knew I wanted to learn. I thought about going to graduate school for a counseling degree. It seemed like the best path forward. My heart was full of compassion and ambition as I sensed the small yet hopefully significant impact that I might have on the world.

When I asked Chris to join me in New York for graduate school he said, "I'm not like you. I need to stay close to my family and friends."

Falling in love with Chris meant living in his world. I wanted to belong to his circle of friends, family, and fraternity so that I could be essential to his life. It was the first of many times that I tried, and failed, to blend into a family that was not my own. The beginning of a painful pattern of trying to find fulfillment in a place I didn't belong.

I applied to graduate schools. Pressure built inside me as two distinct realities—Chris's and mine—tried to coexist within me. I felt like I couldn't hold all the love I felt for Chris and the purpose that I had for my life at the same time. I didn't want to choose between them. I didn't want to be alone. I wanted to be loved, accepted, and taken care of. And I wanted to have the career I knew I was here to have. But I didn't have the slightest idea how to reconcile these seemingly oppositional goals. I was terrified of losing the joy I had found with Chris, petrified of a future without him. Chris could feel me pulling away. He tried harder to convince me to stay, and I felt my faith in the normal, and in happily-ever-after, breaking down. The more I wavered, the more frustrated Chris became.

When I received the envelope from my top choice school, the weight of unbearable responsibility returned. It was so much more than an envelope. It was a decision to abandon Chris or abandon myself.

I stared at the envelope for a long time, uncertain about how I'd make a choice.

I'll leave it up to the gods. If I get in, I go. If I don't, I stay. Let the universe decide my fate.

I opened the envelope with shaky hands. Pale blue print on the top left-hand corner said Teachers College Columbia University, with a crown emblem and an address in New York City.

Congratulations, we would like to....

A rush of joy filled my heart. I couldn't believe I had been accepted. A wave of pain eclipsed the joy as I realized what it meant. I read it over and over. Tears fell on the page. I held it so tightly my fingers left imprints around the perimeter.

I was in love with two opposing forces—Chris and Columbia. I couldn't have both. I felt a tearing, splitting agony at the impending separation. I buried the news and the letter for the moment. We had plans to go to a party. There were dozens of drunk, dancing people. It was the last place I wanted to be. I tried to feign interest, tried to numb my mind, and be the person Chris wanted me to be. I could sense his growing irritation and feel his judgment. We fought about something stupid, and I dashed for the door.

He grabbed my arm. "Don't walk away from me!"

I pulled away in defiance. "Don't touch me!"

That was it. We were done. All the darkness came rushing back. I went to sleep and dreamt of violence.

When I woke in the morning, Chris and I met on the lawn. "I got into Columbia," I said.

His face was blank. He didn't look angry or sad. He didn't even look like he was there. "Congratulations," he mumbled.

I felt a strong pang of disconnection, as if we'd just unplugged from one another.

"You can come with me," I said. It was desperate and pointless.

"What am I supposed to do in New York?"

"Find another job. Pursue singing as a career."

He shook his head.

The burn blazed up my legs and down my arms. My mind spun thoughts of despair.

Then a quiet voice inside said, *Everything is going to be okay. Something is going to happen to you. You don't understand it yet. It will wreck your life as you know it, and then it will all make sense.*

I felt chills on the back of my neck. This was not my voice. I'd never say those things to myself. I looked around suspiciously. If I didn't know better, I would say it was Mom. If it didn't sound so crazy, I would say that she was sitting on the grass next to me.

5

BECOMING AN ADULT IS hard. Becoming an adult while wrestling with psychosomatic trauma symptoms and an ongoing spiritual awakening in a society that requires betrayal of the self for belonging is an impossible odyssey. If my early 20s were a wobbly strut in high heels, my late 20s were a tumble down the rabbit hole into the darkness of the Underworld.

When I separated from Dr. Kelly and Chris after college and moved to New York to pursue my master's degree, I was desperately seeking an identity I could comfortably wear in public. My cultural conditioning was an opposing force to what I knew to be true. There was a growing academic in me, a woman who wanted to uncover the secrets of the mind. She believed in science and patterns and empirical research. A wounded healer was also emerging, a woman who could communicate with the unseen world. She believed in intuition and divinity and her own subjective experience. Soon to appear was the pilgrim, a woman who needed to wander to faraway places to collect pieces of herself in mountains and forests, temples and churches.

While my culture told me I was supposed to fit in a neatly labeled box with one identity, one personality, and one profession, in my bones I felt pulled in multiple directions. Being human is messy and incongruent. We are more paradoxical than we are standardized or uniform.

If anyone had asked me how I felt at 25 years old attending an Ivy League graduate school, I would have said I felt both lucky and unworthy. I was glad to be considered intellectually above-average by the New York elite, and simultaneously wondered when they were going to realize I had no business being there. I bought some pantsuits that would make Hilary Clinton proud. I grew my shaved hair into a cute pixie cut which framed my face in fresh innocence. I subscribed to *The New York Times*, even though I had no interest in the articles. I liked carrying the paper around and flipping through the pages on the subway. It made me feel like a grown-up.

My classmates had honest careers in education or business. They were attending Columbia to get a promotion or make a move up the corporate ladder. I had never had a job other than modeling. I knew how to "look" like a graduate student, but I didn't know how to actually be one.

I dealt with this reality by speaking to as few people as possible. If I didn't say too much, maybe they wouldn't discover I was an imposter. Instead, I buried myself in books. My favorite place to visit was the campus bookstore. I walked down the aisles, stacks of textbooks on either side of me, searching for the names and numbers corresponding to the ones for my courses. It was a sea of information, significant work written by important people. Books had been a lifeline for me during therapy with Dr. Kelly. They taught me a language I could use to communicate with her, and although I was not yet proficient, I was growing more conversant over time - as long as I could keep my emotions at bay. My arms and shoulders ached as I picked up one book after another.

Even though the books were new they seemed somehow old, like they carried the weight of heavy thinking and dense ideas.

During one bookstore visit, a small paperback on a dusty shelf caught my attention. It had a white cover and simple black font which read *Everyday Zen*. I felt pulled toward it, compelled to open it. I read the first page: "If I were to tell you that your life is already perfect, whole, and complete just as it is, you would think I was crazy. Nobody believes his or her life is perfect. And yet there is something within each of us that basically knows we are boundless, limitless."

Whoa, how does that work? This conundrum seemed like an important one to solve. Psychology said I had a disease in my brain which made me excessively worried and gave me panic attacks and nightmares. The doctors said I needed medicine to make me better. The medicine definitely helped.

But the book said I was whole, complete, limitless—that on some fundamental level, I was perfect just as I was. That seemed true, too. But how could both be true? I am sick, and I am well? I am broken, and I am whole? I threw the book on the top of my pile and headed for the checkout counter.

I was enrolled in an accelerated program at Columbia to complete my Master's degree in 12 months. Each course was more challenging than the next. The content was complex and difficult to understand. We were also learning computer skills and programming languages because technology was forecasted to be the way of the future.

As I became more immersed in my coursework, I felt an increasing unease in my mind and body. My neck and jaw were clenched all the time. The rigor of assignments and expectations caused debilitating migraines. I ignored the symptoms, shoved the feelings down as far as possible, and forged ahead. This was a pattern I practiced since childhood. My secrets were heavy, and my body hurt in ways that confused me. I scratched the back of my knees and chewed the inside of my mouth until little pieces of skin came off on my tongue. I was careful to keep the evidence of my pain hidden so that I could blend in with everyone else.

I suppressed the pain successfully until the final weeks of my program, when the pressure became too much. I was on the 1 train heading north to class to take my Organizational Psychology exam when nausea gripped my stomach. My body rocked side-to-side with the sway of the subway. The fluorescent lights and mysterious smells bombarded my senses. I covered my eyes in dark sunglasses and crossed my arms over my lower abdomen. I was grateful for the anonymity of the train and the city in general. No one seemed to care what anyone else was doing. Passengers stepped over bums on the platform like they were cracks in the sidewalk. Unless you were making direct eye contact and exchanging words, you were practically inanimate. When you wanted to be invisible, this was a blessing. When you craved inclusion, this was a curse.

I hobbled out of the station at 125th Street in Harlem. I could see my school, the historic red-brick building, a few blocks away. Between abdominal spasms and cranial cramps, I scurried to my destination. Inside the cool stone walls, students walked fast and determined. I climbed the marble steps in agony, wondering if I was going to make it to the classroom. My mind flooded with questions. *Why am I here? What am I doing? I can't leave. I have to take the exam. I can't stay. I'm falling apart.*

In a flare of clarity, I realized my physical symptoms were so overwhelming that I wouldn't make it through the exam. Tears streamed down my cheeks. I felt lightheaded and scared. My professor's office was a few feet ahead. I stopped in her doorway and cleared my throat to get her attention.

"Excuse me. Can I talk to you for a minute?"

Professor Leah resembled Dr. Kelly in her conservative, polished appearance. She motioned for me to come in. The room was too bright and too white, with piles of paper stacked on the desk. The contrast between old architecture and cheap modern furniture was ugly and disorienting.

I plopped down in a wooden chair. "I'm so sorry," I babbled through my tears. "I don't feel good. Can I miss the test? Can I take it in a few days?" I was mortified at my excessive emotion and blunt request, but I needed to get out of there fast.

She looked shocked. "Are you ok? Did something happen?"

I despised revealing myself to others, especially to strangers. This professor didn't know me. We had never spoken before. I didn't want to disclose anything. I just wanted to avoid the consequences of missing the test and tarnishing my near-perfect GPA.

"Yeah, I'm fine," I said, which must have sounded ridiculous. "I'm just stressed."

"About the exam?" she frowned. "You can't get this stressed about school." She seemed genuinely concerned, a sentiment that surprised me just as much as when Dr. Kelly expressed it.

The heat was rising. I was sweaty and sick. "Okay."

"Take a break. Get some rest. Take care of yourself."

"Okay. Thank you. I'm sorry."

I was genuinely sorry, and embarrassed. I felt weak and insecure and ashamed. I wanted to go home and bury my head under the covers, but I was terrified to face the pain alone. What if there was something seriously wrong with me? What if my appendix ruptured like my mother's? At that thought, I realized couldn't tell the difference between my pain and paranoia. I decided to go to the emergency room.

A quick taxi ride got me to the entrance of North General Hospital. I was admitted quickly and sent to a bed behind a curtain in a room full of beds and curtains. I lay in the fetal position, hands wrapped around my waist, answering the onslaught of questions:

"Are you pregnant?"

"No."

"Do you take any medications?"

"No."

When I got to New York, I had weaned myself off all the meds that Dr. Kelly gave me because I didn't want to be dependent or addicted. Being medicated made me feel like I wasn't strong enough to handle life on my own.

"Do you have any allergies?"

"Please," I whimpered, "The pain is really bad. Is there something you can do?"

I felt the same fever dream descending on me as I did when Mom was sick. The disorientation and chills made it hard to concentrate. There was a flurry of activity and exams. I felt a needle puncture my arm and cool fluids rushing into my veins. A gentle wave of relief washed over me. The less I could feel, the better.

After an indistinguishable amount of time, a tall man in a white coat with a clipboard hovered near the bedside and said, "You have ovarian cysts. One of them probably ruptured. There is nothing we can do."

I heard the words, but I couldn't understand what they meant. Was I dying?

The doctor must have seen the horror on my face. Sweat dripped into my eyes.

"We'll send you home with a prescription," he said. "You should feel better in a couple of days."

I should have felt reassured, but I felt resentful. This wasn't an answer or a solution. I was drugged and exhausted. I had no idea why my body was behaving this way. Anger coursed through my veins like the IV fluids. *What the fuck is going on?* There was a speed and certainty in the people around me. Everyone looked clear and confident about what they were doing. I didn't feel equipped to do "real life" like everyone else. I felt like I was working so hard just to keep my head above water.

I worried that I would always be broken. Maybe so broken that I would end up like the bums on the street.

I was too tired to talk to the doctor. I nodded in compliance. Then I went home and slept for 3 days.

I had to drag myself out of bed the following week to finish my classes. I was also applying to jobs and internships, frantically trying to find a place of belonging in the world. I felt adrift without Dr. Kelly's guidance, and I cast about looking for the next clear sign of direction.

One day, I was taking a break between classes in the student lounge when I saw Susie. She was the only classmate who smiled and made eye contact with me. We had exchanged greetings a couple of times when I complimented her colorful backpack and she said she liked my hair. Susie seemed closer to me in age and personality than the other students, but I couldn't say for sure since we had never hung out. I was curious to learn more about her.

Susie approached me with a crinkled nose. "This place smells terrible," she said.

I laughed out loud. It did smell terrible. They were serving some kind of fish soup that made the room stink like a marina. None of the windows in the old building opened so the stench was inescapable.

"I think it's tuna soup," I said.

"That's gross," she said. "I know this cute coffee shop around the corner. Wanna join me?"

Susie was wearing corduroy pants that flared at the bottom and tea shades reminiscent of Janis Joplin. The edge of a tattoo peeked out from on her ankle. She led me to a French bistro and we settled into soft wicker chairs at a marble-top table. The place smelled like espresso and fresh bread, a significant upgrade from the lounge. Before we ordered, Susie began talking nonstop, beginning with the stress of final exams, followed by the places she liked to eat, her favorite vacation destinations, her dating life, and so on. It was a relief to be with someone who did all the talking and didn't ask me any questions. I let out a big sigh and my shoulders relaxed. I enjoyed the cheery company without any of the anxiety of being exposed. We quickly devoured our cappuccinos and a charcuterie board and returned to school, but not before scheduling a follow-up date.

Susie said she had a friend named George who was a psychic, and that I just had to meet him. George was coming to her apartment that evening and she wanted me to join them. She was so casual in her invitation, as if it was completely ordinary to have friends and psychics congregating in one's apartment.

I was flattered and startled by the invite. I had heard of psychics but had never actually met one. In my mind, they were charlatan women who wore silk robes, hovered over crystal balls, and conned people out of money. I didn't even know that men could be psychics. I was willing to suspend my judgments and attend this clandestine meeting because I enjoyed Susie's company. I figured she would ask George all the questions and he would give her all the answers while I quietly observed. I didn't expect to participate. And I certainly didn't expect my mother to crash the party.

When I arrived at Susie's that night, she was sitting on pillows around a low table with a Latino guy dressed casually in a t-shirt and baggy pants. Her place was exactly what I expected from an Upper West Side apartment—white walls, hardwood floors, narrow hallways, and views of other apartments from every window. But Susie had added her unique character to the place, just as she did with her clothes and conversation. There were eccentric framed photos and colorful tapestries. Collections of hats and books competed for space on her shelves.

"George is giving me a reading," Susie said with glee. They were looking at a deck of cards with pictures of strange characters and symbols.

"Cool." I pretended to know what was happening. I didn't know what a "reading" was, but it must be a good thing if it made her so happy.

"I'll do yours next," he said.

Apprehension washed over me. George was nothing like I expected. He was young and attractive.

"That's ok," I said, "You don't have to."

"I want to." He looked at me with a cool penetrating gaze.

I froze. "Uh, ok," I mumbled.

I settled onto a pillow at the low table. The room was candlelit and warm. Susie wanted to know about her future. George flipped over one card after another and described the meaning to her.

"Ace of Wands. You have a lot of energy, optimism, and confidence to start the next chapter of your life.

"Two of Swords. You will be peaceful and prosperous in pursuit of your goals.

"Three of Cups. There will be an overflowing joy that may even overwhelm you.

"Ace of Swords. You will succeed because of your intelligence, clear thinking, and powerful personality.

"The Sun," he said. "Of course. It all makes sense."

Susie was glowing when he flipped over the last card. The reading didn't mean much to me but they both seemed invested in the divination. There was some conversation and examination of the images. They chit-chatted about the predictions.

I was hoping they had forgotten me, but no such luck. George shuffled the cards and handed me the deck. "Think of a question in your mind." He stared at me again with confident calmness.

I didn't want to think of a question, but there were many buzzing in my head. Questions about school and my career and my shitty physical health. I closed my eyes and held the deck in my hands. It was heavier than I expected. I steadied myself and took a long deep breath.

I just want to know why I'm here. Is there a purpose to my life?

I handed the cards back to George. He shuffled again. One by one, he laid the cards out in front of me.

"The Falling Tower. Something happened. An unexpected loss. It was very destabilizing and made you question everything.

"Three of Swords. It was an important relationship. You feel sad and confused.

"The High Priestess," George frowned. "Did you lose your mother?"

I froze in my seat, unable to speak.

"Oh no," Susie said sadly, as if a cloud had suddenly concealed her light.

George looked at the card again and then back at me, waiting for an answer. There was an awkward pause. I figured I better say something, or the silence would never end.

"Yes," I said. "It was a few years ago."

"You have a spiritual contract with her," he said. "A karmic bond."

The words punctured me like a dozen arrows. I felt sick to my stomach and lightheaded.

"Judgement," George went on. "You're going through an awakening. And you're having health problems."

I couldn't believe he was saying these things. I was so embarrassed. What would Susie think of me now?

"Eight of Wands. Yeah, that makes sense," he said.

"What makes sense?" I asked.

"You've got a lot of change in the future... traveling, too. Not all of it is going to be good. It's going to require a lot of courage. You made a deal with your mom before you were born. She agreed to mentor you from the other side. She is guiding your journey..." He paused again and looked at me, his eyes filled with soft compassion. "But you already knew that, didn't you?"

A jolt of panic hit me like a punch in the gut. *How could he know these things about me?* I wanted to flee, get as far away from George and his evil cards as possible. I felt naked and ashamed.

I nodded. "Yeah."

If I was honest with myself, I'd say it didn't seem like a coincidence I was having the encounter with George, discovering Zen books at the bookstore, or even getting strange sicknesses. It felt divinely guided. Mom appeared to me mostly in nature for the first few years after her death, but then she became a more constant presence, like a spiritual guide. I felt more connected to her after her death than in the 21 years we were physically together. It was as if she was parenting me from the other side.

Sometimes her presence was profound in the way it would bring me the perfect answer just when I needed it. Other times, it was deeply unsettling. I'd been taught that only priests and nuns had a direct line to the divine. I had never heard of this happening to anyone else, and I was afraid of being discovered. Who was I to claim this power?

I was discombobulated for the rest of the evening, counting the minutes until I could make a graceful exit. I should've been grateful for the invitation but I didn't want experiences like that. I wanted to be "normal" and do the ordinary things other twenty-somethings were doing.

I thanked Susie and George on my way out. "See you again soon," I lied.

It was the last time I ever saw them.

6

IN 1999, I GRADUATED magna cum laude from Columbia and landed a cushy job at the US Department of Education in Washington, D.C. It all seemed surreal, like a movie montage where the main character goes from cap-and-gown to U-Haul, cute apartment, and office with a view. For two years, I did my best impression of a government employee with my laminated badge and faux leather briefcase. On the weekends, I explored cafes, monuments, farmers' markets, and other civilized places. I even recruited a geologist named Martin to be my boyfriend. If it weren't for the nagging feeling I was living someone else's life, it would have been heavenly.

The move to Washington DC opened a current of curiosity in me which grew more intense by the day. The US capital was not only extremely diverse in population, but it was also brewing with novel ideas and vigorous campaigning. Every day, I passed by protestors with "Free Tibet" signs, or made small talk with a diplomat from Ghana in the cafeteria line. It sparked a hunger in me to learn more, do more, and devour the world. Little did I know my time in DC would inspire dramatic career changes and travel to a dozen different countries in the next few years.

In the absence of a fixed path or advisor to help me plan, I was left to my own internal guidance to navigate the labyrinth of my physical pain, emotional confusion, and life decisions. I had a profoundly inconvenient intuition that distracted me from my job and compelled me to try the strangest things. At first, it was a series of subversive books which critiqued modern society, especially the education system. I had a natural disdain for authority and delighted in the rebellious material, which was not ideal for my work morale.

Then I volunteered to stuff envelopes at the *International Campaign for Tibet* headquarters and attended a teaching by the Dalai Lama. His regal presence emanated a powerful spiritual energy which was both comforting and confusing. I couldn't comprehend what he was saying in Tibetan, yet somehow, I felt the message he was sending. Eventually, I fell down a rabbit hole of New Age literature about eclectic practices like reiki, yoga, and other "weird" stuff. I was attracted and repulsed in equal measure. My upbringing had taught me not to trust this pseudo-science, but I couldn't help myself. Something about it resonated with me deeply.

In the metaphysical shop where I purchased my illicit books, there was a flyer for an energy healing workshop. It had a photo of hands emanating a prism of light which bore an uncanny resemblance to the optical illusion I saw at Mom's funeral. In all my searching during the previous five years, I had yet to find an explanation for what I'd witnessed. It was a constant source of irritation for me.

I called the number on the flyer and a chipper woman named Victoria invited me to join her class the following weekend. Hoping to find some answers, I agreed to attend.

On Saturday morning, I approached the quaint suburban house with butterflies in my belly. The winding stone pathway was flanked with colorful flowers. The rainbow mat at the threshold was inviting. When Victoria opened the door, I was startled to discover she was nearly a foot shorter than I. She smiled big and welcomed me inside. She reminded me of an eccentric grandmother with hidden powers like the medium in the *Poltergeist* movies. The interior of her home was unassuming. There was plush furniture and a couple of women drinking tea and chatting. We could've been meeting for a knitting club by the looks of things, but I was not there to make friends or craft a scarf. I was there to uncover the secrets of the Universe.

After we settled into the furnished basement with half-dozen massage tables set in rows, Victoria told us her personal story of healing. She had been in a terrible car crash, and Western medicine did nothing to help her. She lay bed for weeks feeling helpless and scared.

"The doctors said I would never walk again," she said. "I did energy healing on myself every day, several times a day, and I was back on my feet in a few months. It's a miracle."

The other women were riveted by the narrative. I was perplexed. Victoria's story contradicted everything I knew about medicine. It sounded radical and suspicious, but she seemed to be walking proof. But how could energy mend the spine and cure paralysis?

We paired off with partners and moved to the tables. Pam, an older woman, laid down face-up and made herself comfortable on the table as I stood nervously at her feet.

Victoria instructed us, "Connect to the energy at the center of the earth. Feel your feet firmly planted on the ground. Draw the energy of the earth up through your feet and into your hands."

I visualized lava coming into my legs. My hands rested gently on Pam's feet. Gradually, I felt warmer and warmer, like someone was turning up the thermostat in the room.

As Victoria guided us through the practice, I moved my hands over various parts of Pam's body every few minutes. Victoria used words like qi, life force, energy field, chakras, and other unfamiliar terms.

The heat in my body expanded. I felt dizzy. My body spontaneously rocked back and forth. I thought I might pass out.

I breathed deeply and tried to focus.

Suddenly, I got a powerful impression that my mom was in the room with me. She felt so close I almost smelled her perfume. It was five years since she died, but somehow, she seemed to be right there with me as if she'd never left. I wondered if I was hallucinating.

Finally, after what seemed like an eternity, Victoria said, "Stop and take a break."

Pam began to weep.

I was startled. I worried I had done something wrong.

Pam took my hand and looked into my eyes. "You have amazing healing hands. The Virgin Mary came to me and wrapped her blue cloak around me. It was the most healing experience I have ever had."

I felt unnerved and stressed out. What did she mean? I wasn't a healer. I hadn't done anything. I had come to the workshop for answers and all I was getting were more questions.

We switched places. I got on the table so Pam could work on me.

She described what she felt as she hovered her hands over my head, chest, and torso. "Your root chakra is blocked. You are not grounded. You are distant from people, and you don't feel safe in the world."

I was shocked by her accuracy.

With closed eyes, she continued to scan me with her hands. "You are carrying a burden that needs to be released. Something painful that needs to be forgiven. It is interfering with the flow of your heart chakra and solar plexus. It's something that makes you feel powerless and vulnerable. Something to do with people you love."

How can she know this by waving her hands over my body?

I felt like I was back in the card reading with George, hearing something from a stranger she couldn't possibly know, and yet she did. I felt the massage bed sway like I was floating on water. It made me uneasy.

When Pam's hands hovered over my throat, she said, "You are not expressing your authentic self. You're afraid of judgment or rejection. You need to speak your truth."

She was blowing my mind.

Then she asked if I would be willing to share my story with her. Without hesitation, I told her about my quest to understand what happened when Mom died. I disclosed my feelings of being an imposter at work and confusion about my life purpose. I felt the words coming out of my mouth as if on automatic pilot. My heart was beating fast and I worried I was rambling.

Pam looked at me intently while she absorbed my words. When I paused, she said, "That must be really hard for you."

She said it with such sincerity, compassion, and empathy that I burst into tears. It felt like a bottomless pit of grief. I wanted it to stop. I was so frustrated with myself for becoming emotional again.

Pam handed me some tissues and sat with me quietly. She had a crown of silvery-white hair and crystal blue eyes. I hadn't really noticed her until that moment. She was almost angelic.

After I regained my composure, she said," You'll figure everything out. You are on the right path."

During the remaining hours of the weekend workshop, Victoria explained the philosophy and methods of energy healing. She talked about taking accountability for our health and activating our innate power of self-healing. She said there were lessons to learn from illness, and practices to bring us closer to enlightenment.

"Not being true to ourselves or loving who we are creates blockages in our energy pathways that manifest as pain and illness in our physical body," she explained. "In order to complete our purpose and transform our soul, we need to clear these blockages and heal the pain and illness."

As the reality of her words set in, I realized there was a lot of healing I needed to do and many lessons I needed to learn if I wanted to feel comfortable in my own skin. It had been so long since I was pain-free, I barely remembered what it was like.

If what Victoria was saying was true, everything I knew about science and medicine was built on a false premise. We weren't biological machines made of mechanical parts disconnected from our hearts, minds and spirits. Illness wasn't something wicked to be cut out or cast out. We were multidimensional beings receiving messages meant to help us. If I accepted this, I would have to rebuild my beliefs from the ground up. I'd have to completely shift my identity and worldview. I had no idea how to do that.

When I left Victoria's house, she invited me back for the Level 2 training. I was already halfway down the rabbit hole. I might as well see where it goes, I thought.

As if on cue, the dubious winds of change blew through my life again. I was laid off from my position at the US Department of Education and simultaneously accepted into a Ph.D. program for Transformative Studies. I was nervous and excited. It felt like everything was coming together and falling apart at the same time. My circumstances seemed random and chaotic on the surface but deep down, it felt like everything might be happening for a reason. It would be years before I understood that my life moved in cycles; things had to fall apart repeatedly in order for me to discover all the pieces of myself. It would be a long time before I could accept the Universe, mysterious in her ways, was always working on my behalf.

Unemployment gave me the freedom to immerse myself in learning 24/7. I took more courses with Victoria and added additional classes in massage therapy, Buddhist meditation, and private sessions with various healers like acupuncturists and nutritionists.

True to my nature, I couldn't just skirt the surface of "alternative medicine." I had to know everything. What was the meaning of my ovarian cysts? Was the body really made of energy? Could energy medicine cure my panic attacks and anxiety? What did all of this have to do with my spiritual experiences? Was Mom causing all of this? The more questions I had, the more motivated I was to answer them.

While I was plumbing the depths of ancient healing methods and Far East philosophy, I also began my doctoral work. I had stumbled onto my Ph.D. program while reading a book called *The Purpose of Your Life* by Carol Adrienne. Carol had helped James Redfield with an experiential guide for *The Celestine Prophecy,* which made her pretty radical in my mind. Our lives had many similarities. She had studied art and psychology. She wrote about living in duality—working in administrative positions and being passionate about spirituality. In the book, she described a program at the California Institute of Integral Studies (CIIS) called Transformative Studies. She said that she followed synchronicities and intuition until she found her life purpose.

"We know that this mysterious life is waiting there for all of us, no matter where we live, no matter what our education happens to be, no matter what kind of childhood we've had. The only thing that matters is that we find a way to open ourselves up to this experience."

Carol's words were another breadcrumb on my life trail. A quick visit to the CIIS website revealed that it was an institution that embodied spirit, intellect, and wisdom. It valued abstract ideas and enigmatic concepts. There were a lot of words in the curriculum description that I didn't understand, like epistemology, ontology, transpersonal psychology, complexity theory, and appreciative inquiry, which only made it more appealing to me.

At CIIS, students were not expected to be good. They were expected to think for themselves, which was the antithesis of my Catholic schooling. CIIS expected students to have original ideas and unique opinions. Classes demanded that participants bring their whole selves to the conversation and use personal experience as the basis for their research. This was astonishing. None of these elements had ever been part of my academic learning before.

As part of my 2-year doctoral program, which was mostly delivered online, we had to attend intensive retreats twice a year with our classmates and instructors. When I booked my travel to California for the first CIIS retreat, I didn't know what to expect. I had never been to California before and had never been on a retreat. I was tense with anticipation. I hoped I would feel a stronger sense of belonging than I had at Columbia, but also be able to keep a safe emotional distance from my classmates.

We were meeting at The Sequoia Retreat Center in Ben Lomond, California, about a 90-minute drive from the San Francisco airport. As the airport shuttle approached a narrow dirt road and turned up a hill into the redwoods, the forest felt peaceful but my insides rumbled with anxiety. Thick trees towered around us, hundreds of feet tall, and covered in red bark. The shuttle stopped in front of a wooden building with vaulted ceilings and big windows. I could smell the smoke from a fireplace burning inside.

I got out of the shuttle and was greeted by a round woman named Bertha. "Welcome to the CIIS intensive!" she said with a smile.

After dropping my bag in my treehouse accommodations, I gathered with sixty people in the meeting room. Bertha rang a brass bowl to quiet the crowd. Everyone stopped talking and moved into a circular formation. My stomach was tight, and my breath was shallow.

We watched in silence as a Spanish woman played the drum and sang a native song for a few minutes. When she finished, Bertha asked each of us to describe one thing we brought to the circle. One by one, each person said their word: passion, joy, love, confidence.

My mind was blank. When I opened my mouth, the word that came out was "courage."

One by one, the faculty members introduced themselves and shared their research interests—altered states of consciousness, expressive arts, Eastern religion, and self-creation.

Robert, my advisor, introduced himself next. "Hi, my name is Dr. Ricci, and my passion is creativity. I'm a musician, and I play the saxophone."

Robert shared details about his background. His mother was Dutch, and his father was Italian. He lived all over the world because his parents were diplomats. He loved living in Lebanon, Greece, and London. He spent a terribly cold year teaching in China in the mountains. He came to America for graduate school about fifteen years ago and loved living here.

With each story, I felt new doors opening in my brain. *I want to travel. I want to live in other countries! How do I do that?* I wondered.

After the introductions, we separated into groups. I met with my cohort—an unusual mix of people including a psychotherapist, a nun, a dietician, a nurse, a consultant, a computer scientist, a physical therapist, a yoga teacher, a minister, an environmentalist, a stay-at-home mom, a grandmother, a shaman, and me. We were not only going to live together for the next five days, but we were also going to be in constant communication in our online classroom for the next 24 months. After that, we would be working on our individual dissertations and presenting our research for review.

As I scanned the faces of my new academic family, I felt weirdly unprepared to be there. I was the youngest cohort member by almost a decade. I was unmarried, had no kids, and no professional resume other than the two years I worked at the Department of Education. Once again, I wondered why I had been admitted and when they were going to realize they had made a mistake.

After lunch, Charles, the shaman, invited us to do a ritual in the redwood grove. The air was crisp, and the ground was an earthy mixture of soil and rain that smelled like incense. Sunbeams streamed through the trees like light shining through cathedral windows. We followed him to a clearing and watched with awe as he visited the trees one by one, offering them shredded tobacco as a gift, sprinkling some of the brown fibers at the base of their trunks.

He asked us to face the East. He closed his eyes and pressed his hands together in a prayer pose. "Great Spirit of the East, warmth of fire and the rising sun, Spirit of the new day and new beginnings, from you comes wisdom, knowledge, and our vital life energy. You purify us and give us clear vision. We give thanks to you and pray that your energy may flow through us for the good of the Earth and all living beings."

He turned to the South and invoked great-grandmother Earth, honoring the grasses, gardens, and flowers. We prayed for peace, renewal, and growth. Turning to the West, he called out to the water spirits and great-grandmother ocean. We gave thanks to the womb of life, the place of dreams, introspection, and the unknown. Finally, he turned to the North, to the great-grandfather sky. "You are vast, wise, and boundless. You bring self-understanding. You give us clarity, strength, and the power to hear inner sounds," he said. We offered prayers and thanks for the last time.

A penetrating silence settled as his words faded away. My body tingled. My breath was full and deep. I felt more comfortable in the silence than when I was forced to interact with my new cohort. I felt relieved by the serenity of the trees and gravity of the Earth.

After a few minutes, Charles told us to touch the trees, to feel their life force. I found a tree and put my hands on the rough surface. I could feel the strength and stability, the power that kept this being standing for more than one hundred years. I understood how ancient people could worship in a place like this. This was the church before there were churches. This was the stone buildings of my youth, the mystical experience of Mom in the caterpillar, and the history of ritual, all rolled into one.

When the ceremony was over and I returned to my room, I felt utterly exhausted and drained but something subtle had shifted. More light was seeping through the cracks in my armor. I was opening myself up to the experience. I was embracing the change. CIIS gave me new possibilities and invited me to become a new person. It was up to me whether or not I would surrender my mask and let go of the things holding me back. I had spent a lifetime keeping my private thoughts private and my history buried. I felt exposed and vulnerable revealing myself to strangers. Even if they supported me and validated my ideas, I still felt fragile and timid.

The retreat's various healing sessions and massage classes moved the emotions through my body when they bubbled to the surface. During one session with a friend, Jolie, she pushed gently on my neck and shoulders, releasing layers of tension and stress. I felt my body getting softer and my limbs getting lighter.

Sabine, the massage instructor, led Jolie through the routine, reminding her which strokes to do—effleurage, petrissage, cross-fiber friction. Jolie glided her hands along my spine as she encouraged me to breathe deeply. She touched one area on my back near my spine. It was tender and achy. She held her hand still. A warm sensation spread through my back, subtle at first, and then growing in temperature and pressure. Jolie wasn't letting up, but she wasn't pushing harder, either. She was just holding me in a steady, consistent way.

Suddenly, incredible grief rose from my belly into my chest, throat, and face. I burst into tears, sat up, and covered my face with the sheet.

"Oh my God! Did I hurt you? What happened? Why are you crying?" Jolie wiped sweat from her brow with the back of her hand. Her eyes were wide with a stunned expression.

My body rocked with sobs. I tried to catch my breath. I wanted to tell her that I was okay, but I couldn't get the words out.

Sabine rushed over. She put one hand on Jolie and one hand on me. "It's okay. It's an emotional release."

"Emotional release?" Jolie looked terrified.

"Yes, it's common for people to release emotion during a massage. The body stores memories and feelings in the tissues. If the client is holding onto something painful, it will come out when you touch her."

"Are you okay?" Jolie asked me again.

I still couldn't speak, so I nodded.

Sabine said, "She's okay. She's a strong girl."

She looked at me and smiled. "Right?"

I *was* strong. But I was also tired. This kind of incident had been happening over and over. It happened when the chiropractor adjusted my spine and when the acupuncturist tapped needles into my skin. It happened in a consultation with my doctoral advisor and in a benign journaling workshop. My emotions did not discriminate. They had no sense of social rules or appropriate behavior. No matter where I went or who I was with, they could burst out at any moment, demanding my attention. It was terribly frustrating, and I was awfully insecure about it. Sometimes people reacted like Jolie—alarmed and confused. Other times, if the practitioner had the necessary training, there was mild acknowledgement and reassurance, "You're doing a great job," which only made me feel pitiful and patronized.

More than anything, I wanted to have a breakthrough. I wanted to know where all of this was coming from, and how to get rid of it. It had been more than 20 years of panic, anxiety, nightmares, and other symptoms. *How much more was I going to have to endure?*

7

AFTER NEARLY 1,000 HOURS of training in massage therapy and energy medicine, I accidentally became a healer. I did not set out to pursue a career in medicine. I did not want to follow in my father's footsteps. I tried to move as far as possible in the opposite direction. I watched my father struggle through medical training, residency, starting a practice, and dealing with patients. I sat on his hip in my mini-sailor dress when he walked across the stage of his graduation from Hershey Medical School, and I was there when the medical board threatened to take away his license less than a decade later because of repeated complaints about his bad behavior. I saw how the pressure made him violently angry and unhealthy. Being a healer was the furthest thing from my mind.

In addition, "medicine" never helped me very much. Whenever I was sick or injured, I was immediately put on antibiotics or other medication, and I spent a significant amount of time in hospitals and doctors' offices for every possible ailment. During my parents' divorce, I had stomach aches and headaches from the stress of separation. I was sent for an MRI (a diagnostic test to look for brain damage) and a GI scope (a procedure where they put a long tube down the esophagus to look for gastrointestinal damage).

Even Dr. Kelly gave me four different psychiatric medications when I complained of emotional pain. The human factor—a person in distress—was overlooked for the preferred medical explanation of symptoms.

My traditional Catholic upbringing and medical background offered no explanation for the mystical experience I had at Mom's funeral or the subsequential mysterious interactions I had with George, Pam, and others. The conventional medical paradigm said illness is something to be removed or cured. Healing is a defined, rational, and planned process, and the physician/healer knows what's best for the patient. This belief system puts all of the knowledge, power, and responsibility in the hands of the treater. The patient is nothing more than a body in need of repair. Needless to say, this approach left me feeling powerless and distraught.

Gradually, as I continued taking classes and workshops in Alternative Medicine, I acquired a new set of beliefs—many of which were the opposite of my former assumptions. In some respects, it was as if the pendulum had swung to the other extreme. Some of my new beliefs included: healing is a mysterious process that is more an art than a science, illness is purposeful and carries a spiritual message, the knowledge, power, and responsibility for healing lie within the patient, and healers are more than scientists because they facilitate the spiritual growth of their patients.

I became aware that a healer could have a transformative relationship with a patient where both individuals were changed as a result of their interaction. The lines between who was giving, receiving, doing, and causing the healing were blurred. The lines between physical, mental, emotional, and spiritual health became fuzzy. The process of healing and the role of the healer were much more open, diverse, complex, paradoxical, and ambiguous.

Studying energy medicine and massage therapy made me feel at home in the medical community for the first time—even if it was an "alternative" medical community. Even with this new sense of belonging, however, it was sometimes scary to be immersed in a new world. I heard bizarre stories about astral travel, talking to spirits, and memories of past lives. I was mesmerized, but there was also something foreboding about them. They seemed forbidden, dangerous, ominous—like the kind of witchcraft that would have gotten you burned at the stake 300 years ago. I never felt completely at ease in the esoteric realms. I hoped that with time and practice, I might shake the distress and own my own powers.

For my final Healing Touch workshop, the method of energy medicine I first learned from Victoria, in 2002, I gathered with a dozen women in a cozy retreat center in Virginia. The room was filled with rocking chairs and pillows. Our teacher, Mary Jo, introduced herself and told us she had been part of Healing Touch for fifteen years. She was tall, strong, and graceful like a mountain, the kind of woman who made me feel safe and contained.

In preparation for the weekend, we had to compile photos, resumes, certificates, and personal mementos which described our journeys to becoming healers. I collected everything from my university diplomas to a picture of my "very big aura" taken by an aura photographer at a New Age Expo and arranged it all neatly in plastic sleeves in a leather binder.

Mary Jo explained we would share our portfolios with each other. I felt nervous about that. I hoped I wouldn't burst into tears as I did in so many similar situations.

Mary Jo began by telling us about her journey. She heard voices when she was a teenager which told her to become a nurse. After she became a nurse, the voices told her she would do spiritual work and help the aborigines in Australia. She became involved in energy medicine after about twenty years of nursing. She began traveling the world, meeting healers from other cultures, having premonitions about past lives, and channeling stories from sacred objects. It sounded like a fairytale or science fiction movie, but it also unsettled me. Was it the same for all healers? Was I going to be plagued by unusual voices, premonitions, and other supernatural occurrences if I stayed on this path?

When Mary Jo finished talking, the other women shared. One woman got on the path because of an illness. Another had a spontaneous kundalini awakening, where the dormant energy rises from the base of the spine all the way up to the seventh chakra, or energy center, at the top of the head. A third woman met her spiritual guides during a meditation. They told her where to go and what to do. I believed everything these women were saying, but it was hard to accept it as truth. No matter how many mystical stories I heard, something inside of me resisted fully believing.

When it was my turn, I hesitantly explained the spiritual connection I had with my mother after she died, discovering meditation and Buddhism, reading esoteric books, and the energy classes with Victoria, which led to massage school and my Ph.D. program, where I chanted in the forest with a shaman, and so on.

I felt surprised at how much had happened in such a short amount of time. Just a few years earlier I'd left modeling in New York with no sense of direction or purpose. Now it seemed like something much bigger was governing my life. When my classmates complimented me on my presentation, I deflected and rejected their praise.

Even though I was smart, talented, powerful, and beautiful, I didn't know it. I believed I wasn't as good as all the other teachers, speakers, writers, and healers in the world. I had everyone else on such a pedestal. I thought there was no way I was ever going to be at their level. I had not yet become a woman, even though I was 28 and had a master's degree from Columbia. I looked like a woman on the outside, but on the inside, I still felt like a small, insignificant child. The nasty internal monologue accusing me of being a worthless fraud wasn't as loud, but the message still played subliminally in the background.

After the presentations, Mary Jo met with each of us privately to discuss our progress. When I entered the small office for my appointment, Mary Jo looked comfortable and relaxed in her big velvet chair. I sat on the small wooden chair in front of her, feeling nervous and insecure. Mary Jo reassured me I had done an excellent job on my portfolio. She said I had the potential to be a powerful healer if I overcame some of my limitations.

"There are two areas where you need to grow," she said. "First, you need to acknowledge yourself more and not be dismissive of your accomplishments."

This caught me off-guard. "I didn't want to sound like I was bragging," I said.

I was embarrassed that she called me out.

"It's not bragging when you confidently share your experiences. It inspires and empowers other people."

"Okay."

"The second thing has to do with your father. You need to forgive and heal that relationship."

Seriously? I thought. This is her feedback?

"My father?" I asked incredulously.

"Yes. You mentioned him negatively during your portfolio presentation."

"I did? I don't even remember that."

The outrage I carried about my father was so ingrained it was as much a part of me as my eye color or hair. I'd been mad at him for as long as I could remember, and I didn't expect that to ever change.

"It's probably an unconscious habit, but it's important you change it because you can only take people as far as you've gone. If you're holding onto resentments, you cannot help others meet those same challenges."

Mary Jo's words were sharp, and I felt scolded. I couldn't believe she expected me to forgive my father. I had no intention of doing that. What was the point, anyway? I wasn't ever going to see him again. I'm sure the gods were laughing at me that day, saying amongst themselves, "If only she could see what's coming next."

As I moved toward certification in Healing Touch and massage therapy, I completed hundreds of sessions with patients. I delivered healing treatments to men, women, old, young, end-of-life, and prenatal babies. I learned how to use my hands to direct energy flow throughout the body to promote healing and balance.

As I followed the prescribed pattern from ankle to knee, knee to hip, hip to belly, belly to heart, and heart to head, I fell into a sort of trance. I was immersed in a feeling of energized focus, fully enjoying the gentle movements. Something in the person's body told my hands where to go, how long to stay there, and when to move on to the next spot. Sometimes I perceived sensations or emotions through unspoken language between the client and me. It felt natural and effortless.

In my final exam for massage therapy certification, my instructor required me to give her a blindfolded massage. On a warm afternoon in May, Sabine climbed onto my table. Her body was long, narrow, and strong. I covered my eyes with a scarf then undraped her back. I stood at the front of the table, near her head, and felt my feet connecting to the earth beneath me. Slowly and gently, I glided my hands down her back, feeling each fiber of the muscles and every raised vertebra along the way. I kneaded her shoulders, neck, and upper back, listening to her body talking to me, telling me what to do. Even though my eyes were closed, I knew how much pressure to use, and how long to stay in certain areas.

I dropped into the energy of her body like sinking into a pool of warm water. I was transported to a spacious, timeless place of pure feeling and sensation. Moving around the table, I followed a flow and rhythm like the rise and fall of the breath. I stayed in this transcendent space for the entire sixty minutes.

When I finished the massage, Sabine complimented me on my work. "You found every one of my spots. You'll make a good therapist."

Even though I appreciated her comment, I didn't need her to say it. I felt more confident about giving massages than I had felt about anything in my life. Maybe it wouldn't be so hard to be a healer after all.

In 2002, after I completed the requirements for my massage license, I packed up my belongings, including a brand-new massage table, and drove south to Florida. Miami had been summoning me ever since a spring break visit in college, where I stayed out all night dancing and watching the sunrise on the beach. I hoped the tropical climate and turquoise waters would give me a new perspective and fresh energy. Miami was also a more popular spa destination than DC, so it seemed like a good idea for my new career.

Driving across the causeway to South Beach, I gasped at the mega-mansions and million-dollar yachts. Miami was the most beautiful city I had ever seen. I settled into a sweet 1-bedroom apartment in an art deco building a few blocks from the beach, where gorgeous girls in thong bikinis and shirtless boys with glistening skin gathered for sunbathing and volleyball games. A week later, I got a gig at a local spot called *Massage by Design*, with a steady stream of rich and famous clients. Miami customers had an infinite amount of money to spend on pleasuring themselves. For a short time, every part of my body felt at ease, and the critical commentary in my mind was quiet.

At first, I did one or two treatments a week, but soon I did 3 or 4 a day. I also provided resources and support for self-care, life transitions, stress management, and personal growth. I tried to balance my approach to include both Western medicine and Alternative Medicine. I restrained from saying too much about "energy" or things like "chakras", for fear of being seen as a "woo-woo" quack, even though I didn't see my teachers that way. I didn't want to be a doctor like my father, and I didn't even like modern medicine, yet I maintained some conviction that it was superior to Alternative Medicine.

My experiences heightened my curiosity and propelled me even deeper. I wanted a clearer understanding of my chosen profession. I also wanted to contribute something to the literature for others who shared a similar interest. I had completed the first two years of my doctoral education, and it was time to select a dissertation topic. I decided to research female healers. Since Alternative Medicine was still in its infancy, information about contemporary women healers was difficult to come by. I planned to talk to different types of healers from diverse backgrounds and cultures, which gave me an excuse to travel to other countries. I secretly hoped to meet older, wiser women who could give me insights and guidance. I wanted to learn from them.

I spent my first year in Miami vacillating between serious dissertation preparations on the computer and increasing indulgences in the city's many seductions. Miami is a world of shiny objects. It begs you to enjoy life to the fullest. Anything you want—from love affairs to exotic cars—is at your fingertips. If you're a young, beautiful woman, it's even more accessible. All I had to do was walk into a restaurant and within minutes, men were buying me drinks, and dinner, and inviting me back to their homes or hotel rooms. For someone like me who needed a lot of stimulation and attention, it was irresistible. I wasn't into drugs or alcohol, but I didn't need them in Miami. I could get my fix with all-night Latin beats, last-minute trips to the Keys, shopping sprees, and romantic infatuations.

If I were a healthy, happy woman, Miami might have been a godsend, but I didn't know who I was. There was no solidity to me. I was a free spirit, completely ungrounded. I had no sense of home or roots or center of gravity. I didn't know what was true for me. I grasped, reached for, sought out, and experimented with an insatiable urgency.

I was whirling, caught in a storm of ideas and inspiration, but also easily overwhelmed. The energy would grow so strong I would get really wired and be unable to sleep. I'd stay up all night reading and writing, give massages all day, and then go out dancing until I crashed in exhaustion.

Summertime in Miami is a reprieve from the busy tourist traffic because it's too hot and humid to be outside most days. In the summer of 2003, the flow of clients at *Massage by Design* slowed, which was a blessing for some. But I didn't want to slow down. I wanted to speed up. I packed a backpack and boarded a plane to Europe. I planned to visit eight countries in eight weeks. I had many motivations, from seeing a guy that I liked in London, to learning about cultural medicine in different places, to making a pilgrimage to sites Mom had wanted to visit but never did. I had a bucket list of destinations—some touristy ones like the Sagrada Família Basílica in Barcelona and the Giza pyramids in Egypt, and other sentimental ones, like the Irish countryside and African safari, Mom's top two most-talked-about attractions.

On the plane from Miami to Dublin, I flipped through the pages of *Earthwalking Skydancers*, a book about women healers. Each chapter was an exploration of pilgrimages to sacred places known for their feminine energy and goddess spirituality, such as the Chalice Well of Glastonbury, and the Temple of Athena.

The author wrote about Old Europe and how it used to be a mecca of female healers who practiced herbal medicine and midwifery. After centuries of peaceful existence, the Catholic Church killed an estimated one million of these "witches" for their evil witchcraft. The thought of being murdered for what I was practicing was horrifying, and I wondered how much of that history had to do with my reservations. It felt like the trauma of that persecution might still be alive within me.

As the green pastures of Ireland emerged outside the airplane window, a vibrant rainbow crossed the sky. I remembered an Irish lullaby about Killarney that Mom used to sing to me when I was a kid. It had been twenty years since Mom sang that song to me, and seven years since I'd heard her sing anything at all. I felt her traveling with me, even though her body was long gone. It was strange to feel so far away from her and yet so close to her at the same time.

I wandered the cobblestone roads of Dublin. Crowded pubs on every block were filled with smiles, conversation, and clinking pints of Guinness. I boarded a bus for a tour of the country, and my heart swelled with joy. Hills and farms rolled by as flutes, fiddles, and bagpipes on the speakers played a synchronized soundtrack to the landscape.

We visited ancient Celtic ruins, abandoned stone monasteries, and ceremonial burial mounds over five thousand years old. It felt like the sacredness of the land was oozing through the moss. I marveled at the coastal towns with their stoic lighthouses and salty, damp air. I meditated on the dark rocks and crashing water. I drifted off to sleep with green and foggy countryside flowing through my mind.

On one of the overland drives, Caroline, our guide, passed around a microphone and asked us to share something about ourselves.

I listened to each story with curiosity until the microphone was in my hand. I had butterflies in my belly. "Ugh...I'm not good at this. I don't really know what to say... I came to Ireland because my mother died seven years ago, and she always wanted to see this country but never had the opportunity. I'm here on a sort of pilgrimage for her."

My words were met with silence. I could hear my heart beating. I returned the mic to Caroline. She had blue watery eyes.

"That's beautiful," she said softly in her Irish accent.

On our last day of the tour, Caroline announced that we would be stopping in Killarney for the night.

Killarney was the town Mom used to sing about. I felt a surge of nostalgia and nervous anticipation of what it would be like to connect with the fairytale place of my lullabies.

After checking in, a few of us visited a pub where an Irishman was playing Celtic songs on a guitar. I told Caroline how my mom used to sing the lullaby to me. She said, "You should ask him to sing it."

"I can't." I didn't think I could handle hearing it.

"Then I will."

Caroline whispered something to the musician. He nodded. She sat back down next to me with a big smile.

The performer strummed the guitar sincerely. An ethereal sound filled the room. I closed my eyes.

"Over in Killarney many years ago...."

I was a child again, in my bed, under the covers, cat curled up at my feet, both of us dozing to the sound of Mom's song.

"My mother sang a song to me in tones so sweet and low...."

Mom was alive. The cat was alive. We were all alive and bound together in the melody.

"Just a simple little ditty in her good old Irish way...."

I was drenched in emotion. He was singing my pain, my loss, my pilgrimage.

"I'd give the world if I could hear her sing that song today...."

When the song faded to silence, my eyes and face were wet with tears. I'd never felt so close and so far away from home at the same time.

After bittersweet goodbyes with Caroline and a few of my fellow travelers, I caught a train to South England to visit the mythical land of pagan priestesses. As I approached the city of Glastonbury, my whole body vibrated. I strolled along stone paths through lush gardens to the Chalice Well. According to legend, the well sprang from the ground when the Holy Grail was placed inside. I was mesmerized by the reddish water. Locals believed it had magical powers. I felt some force of natural beauty running through me as I peered down into the water.

I wandered the ancient town and stumbled into a healing center covered with pink and purple morning glory vines. A friendly lady escorted me into a small, fragrant treatment room decorated with sparkling crystals and flickering candles. As she moved her hands around my body, I fell into the crack between awake and asleep. Visions of goddesses, one after the other, appeared in my mind. Persephone and Demeter walking through wheat fields. St. Bridget pouring water from her hands. Triple Moon Goddesses surrounded by angels. The images were like a gateway to another world. I felt connected and supported by them; like they were part of the guiding force on my journey.

When I left the center, my head was spinning with everything I had seen. I spent a few more days exploring the prehistoric stone circle of Stonehenge and the hot springs of Bath. With each step forward, I felt like I was moving farther back in time, and farther away from my life in Miami. I was finding myself and losing myself simultaneously, unable to hold firmly to one identity, one version of myself that made sense. I wondered if I would ever have the certainty and stability that others seemed to feel. *Would I ever be whole?*

As I traveled the 15+ hours from South England to South Africa, I journaled about my experience, writing many poems and stories and drawing pictures of goddesses that came to me in my visions. I felt myself transported into a wonderfully weird state of mind, falling deeper down the rabbit hole of feminine mysteries. I felt alive and electric, and less concerned about whether or not I appeared odd to others.

The first thing I heard when I landed in Johannesburg was the tribal beats of the dark continent. They were native and raw, like the vibrant prints on the ebony people. I jumped in a van with a group of people who were heading north to Victoria Falls. A couple of hours into the drive, we stopped for a hike through a lush and misty rainforest. Exotic plants and wildlife surrounded the steep footpath. When we reached God's Window, a panoramic view over canyons, rock formations, and waterfalls three thousand feet above the forest floor, I was speechless. It was the most beautiful place in the world.

After an overnight stay in a tribal village, we headed to Kruger National Park for a safari. Hundreds of buffalo and vultures surrounded us as we drove through the park in an open-air jeep. A herd of elephants crossed the road in defiance of our presence. Lions lounged in the shade, waiting for nightfall when they could stalk their prey in darkness. I felt transported to a time before civilization, when beasts ruled the land and humans hid in caves. The earth seemed more powerful and magnificent than ever before.

By the time we got to Victoria Falls, I was madly in love with Africa. I wished Mom was physically with me. I wanted to see the look on her face, the sparkle in her eye. I wanted this to be a moment between us that I could hold in my heart. That was never going to happen. I didn't know how I felt about it. After all, I probably wouldn't have made the trip if Mom hadn't died. I hoped she was happy that I'd made it that far. I hoped my journey was enough for both of us. Little did I know this was only the beginning of our nomadic adventures together.

8

WHEN I RETURNED TO Miami in the fall of 2003, the city was a shock to my senses. I thought I would feel relieved to be home after living out of a suitcase for eight weeks, but I didn't. Miami felt chaotic, loud, and uncomfortable. The salty humidity was suffocating. There was no one waiting for me to return—no family or significant other, just a pile of dissertation paperwork and a long line of wealthy clients who wanted me to make them feel better.

I tried to resume my normal life, but I had an emotional hangover from my travels, which was heavy and draining. I was so lost. I didn't want to miss my mother. I didn't want to be the weirdo who believed in angels and legends. I desperately wished there was something I could do to fast forward to a time when things wouldn't hurt so much; when I wouldn't feel confused or stressed. Or at least, when the intensity of it all would be diminished.

I sat for a couple of days in my dark apartment, wondering what to do with myself. I was too stubborn or too scared to face the pain buried in my fragile heart. I couldn't stand to be alone with myself. I needed to feel different. I yearned for distraction.

I couldn't ask for help. I wasn't good at knowing who to trust. I had been conditioned to tolerate such bad behavior that I didn't have a good radar or high standards. I unconsciously accepted people who behaved poorly as normal.

I tried to ignore my emotions and focus on my dissertation, but when I sat at my computer I was paralyzed and unable to write. When it came to expressing my beliefs or ideas, I felt like there was a noose around my neck. I was adept at regurgitating the ideas of others, but I didn't have anything worthwhile to say.

I looked at the academic books scattered around me and began to cry. These people are geniuses, I thought. I was equal parts desperate aspiration and paralyzing insecurity. Then I felt bad about feeling bad because everything I was learning told me to be grateful, humble, count my blessings, and shit like that.

I didn't feel blessed. I felt cursed. Why couldn't I just be normal like everyone else? I begged the gods to fix me or leave me alone.

The gods didn't respond.

Fuck it, I thought, I'll fix myself.

I wanted to change everything—my hair, my face, my body. I wanted to be a different person. Over the next few months, I went on a dramatic diet. I gave up all sugar and junk food and went through delirious withdrawal symptoms. I sweated out the toxins at boxing classes, dance classes, and kundalini yoga classes—one of my newest obsessions.

I went to the salon with a tousled mess of dark brown hair and emerged with shiny golden locks cascading down my back. I walked into a shopping center wearing a t-shirt, ripped jeans, and flip-flops and left in a miniskirt, tank top, and heels. I got breast implants and a few more tattoos around my ankle and lower back.

I received a surge of attention for my transformation that inflated my ego and fueled my desire for more. It was an easy way to forget the pain, a pattern that kept me hovering just above the psychic darkness. New romantic excitement and being sexually desirable were welcome distractions. I had no idea that the patterns of my romantic affairs—and their instability—could lead to my unraveling.

I found a new boyfriend, who love-bombed me with tickets to rock concerts and road trips in his red Porsche. For my 30th birthday, I did Ecstasy (MDMA) with him for the first time, pushing new limits, and breaking more boundaries in search of a greater high. I was endlessly seeking, distracting, grasping, and avoiding. The pressure was building, but I didn't want to listen. To stop moving would have dropped me on the tracks in front of a speeding train of pain.

At the end of the year, Porsche boyfriend whisked me off to Asia. My persistent nagging motivated him to plan the trip. It was summertime again in Miami. I feared being bored, and I was sure that the secrets to happiness were buried in some temple or cave in the Far East.

Buddha was enlightened, wasn't he? I thought. I'll just do whatever he did.

Again, I planned eight countries in eight weeks, starting in Thailand and ending in Tibet. My boyfriend could stay for the first month. Then he had to return to work while I finished the trip.

I did not find enlightenment in Bangkok. It was loud and smoky, crowded with taxis, tuk-tuks, and millions of people. It looked like one large market of glitzy shopping malls and roadside stalls serving Thai food. At night, the streets were filled with thousands of young girls dressed in provocative outfits next to signs that said, "You like sexy ladies?" Many of these girls were trafficked by criminal gangs. It made me sick to my stomach, but I was too focused on finding salvation for myself to save anyone else.

Cambodia did not deliver spiritual solace either. The streets of the Phnom Penh buzzed with locals riding mopeds, with chickens and pigs strapped to the handlebars. A local tour guide told us stories of the killing fields where the Khmer Rouge regime murdered more than a million people from 1975 to 1979. Some victims were required to dig their own graves. Children and infants were murdered by being bashed against trees. I did not want to feel the grief or trauma of the people. I snapped photos of the jungle ruins of Angkor Wat and pretended everything was fine.

I was weary and depleted when we arrived in Bali, desperate for some blissful rejuvenation like I had seen in the brochures. Unfortunately, our visit corresponded with the Saka New Year. The Hindus were carrying giant monster dolls through the streets, representing the negative aspects of society and living things. The parade ended with countless bonfires, where the monsters were burned and fell to ashes in the cemetery.

Following the procession, Bali went into complete lockdown for twenty-four hours. People were forbidden to leave their houses or turn on any lights or music. The silence was deafening.

How did I manage to find monsters on the most beautiful island in the world? I wondered. It felt like some kind of cosmic joke.

It was time for my boyfriend to return to the US. Suddenly I was scared about being alone in Asia. "Can you stay with me?" I asked.

"You can take these if you feel anxious." He handed me a bottle of Klonopin, a powerful prescription sedative.

It had been years since I'd taken pharmaceuticals. I had been white-knuckling my way through my anxiety and panic. I didn't want the pills, but it was better than nothing. I had another month of travel, and I wasn't sure I could survive on willpower alone.

I took one of the pills when I boarded the flight to Delhi, and another when I landed. Being groggy was better than feeling my feelings.

When I stepped out of the airport in India, I was assaulted by thousands of beggars and haunting poverty, the likes of which I had never seen. An infant lay on the sidewalk, a tourist trap for money. A man with no eyes crawled on all fours around me. I was surrounded by crippled children, blind children, and desperate children. They were everywhere, hands outstretched, saying, "Dollar. Dollar." If Thailand and Cambodia were offensive, India was repulsive.

I was crying when I checked into my hotel. The swirling paranoia of a panic attack descended on me, darkness closing in on all sides. I felt fragile and nauseous. What am I going to do? I thought. This is all too much.

I summoned the courage to go outside the next day. The smell in the streets was so rancid I used my shirt to cover my mouth and nose to keep from vomiting. Bloated dead bodies floated on the surface of the Ganges while thousands of people bathed in the water. The shore was crowded with holy temples. Devotees chanted and played music. My mind ping-ponged in a thousand directions. *Oh God, make it stop!* I was unraveling. I took another Klonopin, and then another.

Determined to salvage the trip. I pushed through to Agra, Puna, Goa, and Bodhgaya. Each day, I felt a little sicker and more depressed. I was existing on bread, soda, and Klonopin—none of which was helping my condition.

Standing under the Bodhi Tree where the Buddha became enlightened, I felt the rush of my mother's presence again. I felt her in the air, in the leaves, in the breeze. It didn't make me feel better, it just reminded me of how I was never going to see her again, even though she was stalking me everywhere I went.

I will have to keep running. I will never be able to stop running.

For the grand finale, I planned to travel overland from Kathmandu to Lhasa. I was supposed to have a few days of rest in Nepal before the trek, but while I was sleeping the first night, I heard banging on the door. Then a voice shouted, "We have to leave immediately. The Chinese are going to close the border. You won't be able to get out of Nepal."

In a terrified rush, I jumped in a jeep with the tour guide and a couple from Germany. We drove for hours and finally stopped for the night around midnight at a roadside shack. Bugs crawled over the floors, the walls, and the bed in the frigid room. The bathroom was a hole in the ground behind the building, and running water was nowhere to be found. It was so cold I could see my breath. I slept in my clothes on a dirty mattress for a few hours.

When the sun came up, we headed for the border crossing. The Chinese guards were menacing and aggressive. Waiting made my stomach churn. When we finally got into Tibet, I was wrecked. I thought maybe we could stop and recover but we were transferred to another van and the driver took off like a madman, racing up the mountain on a narrow dirt road. A truck came barreling toward us. We skidded to the edge and nearly slid off the 200-foot cliff.

I shook all over and started to hyperventilate. The German lady yelled at the driver, "Slow down! Slow down!"

The driver pulled back onto the road, tearing through a landscape that looked as desolate as the surface of Mars. He didn't slow down. He didn't care. We climbed to a fifteen-thousand-foot mountain pass, and my head nearly exploded.

After hours of nauseating motion, we stopped at a village and unloaded our stuff into another shack. Even though I was wrapped in a sleeping bag and wearing all my clothing, I was freezing and couldn't sleep.

When the sun came up, I was terrified to get back in the car, but I forced myself to get in anyway. The driver took off on the same insane ride. It was a roller coaster of emotion and sickness. I had flashbacks of Mom and Dad fighting, Mom locking me in that room the time I'd stayed out so late at night. I felt trapped, with no way out. The rumble was rattling my body and mind.

When we stopped at the next town, I refused to get back in the car. "I'm not going."

The guide and couple looked at me like I was crazy.

"You can't just stay here in the middle of nowhere," the German girl said to me.

My jaw clenched. "I'm not spending one more day in a car with that driver."

"But what will you do?" she asked.

"I'll figure it out."

They drove away, leaving me alone in the middle of Tibet.

I asked the people on the street if anyone could drive me to Lhasa. I didn't speak Tibetan. They didn't speak English. It was a game of sign language and broken phrases.

A man driving a van with a dozen Tibetan men inside offered to take me. I climbed into the passenger seat. I looked out the window, hoping for some sight of comfort, but the passing landscape was covered with abandoned monasteries, and sanctuaries that used to have thousands of monks before the Chinese kidnapped or murdered them.

We stopped at a construction zone where the Chinese military, dressed in green uniforms, were pointing big rifles at Tibetan slaves laying the cement for new roads. The driver bribed a guard so that we could keep going.

I am so scared, I thought. I am scared for myself. I am scared for the world. This is the worst trip of my life.

Finally, eight hours after I got into the van, we arrived in Lhasa. I laid in bed for a few days shaking and crying until I boarded my flight to go home.

When I landed back at the Miami airport, a text message on my phone said, *Gabrielle, someone broke into your apartment.*

Shell-shocked, I made it home. I entered my apartment, stood in front of the desk where my computer used to be, and bawled my eyes out.

I called my boyfriend.

"I can't stay here," I cried.

"You can stay with me," he said.

When I got to his place, his ex-girlfriend was sleeping on the couch.

I was so disoriented I crawled into his closet, lay on the floor, and tumbled down a vortex of pain in my mind.

Sex slaves. Genocide. Bonfires. Monsters. Beggars. Dead Bodies. My mother. My father. Rumbling. Rattling. Trapped. Broken.

A mind-numbing migraine settled on me. I was twitching and shaking. Opposing forces inside of me were waging war while disparaging commentary flooded my mind: *Who am I? What am I doing? I am nothing. I am nobody.*

I felt my childhood wounds surfacing. I was angry. I wanted to channel all of my rage into my fists and punch something so hard it would break my arms. There was nothing to punch. There was nobody there.

A day and night went by. I stayed on the closet floor. My boyfriend didn't talk to me or touch me. I felt ashamed and humiliated. More insanity tore through my mind: *I am so alone in the world. What am I going to do?* Mountains of impassable, impenetrable pain surrounded me on all sides. Like shoveling the snow in a blizzard, each little bit I removed was replaced with more falling from the sky. I didn't know what was happening or why I couldn't pull my shit together. No matter how hard I tried, it felt like I was drowning in quicksand. I didn't want to feel anything, but there was a storm of emotion moving through me.

I don't want to be here, I thought. Not only did I not want to be in Miami, but I also didn't want to be in my body, I didn't want to be on the planet.

I was still on the floor when the sun went down and came up again. What's wrong with me? I wondered. Terrible memories flooded like someone had opened every locked door in my mind and let all the demons out. I felt little stabbing pinches, like bug bites, all over my body.

The rhetoric raged on in my mind. *I am so inadequate, so helpless. I'm so sorry all of the time. Sorry that I can't do better. Sorry that I couldn't stop my father. Sorry that I couldn't save my brother. I'm sorry that I'm still so broken and trying to put my pieces together.*

I lost track of the days in the closet. I fantasized about drowning in the ocean, and how the pain would finally end. I was spiraling and descending into nowhere.

I want to walk out onto the water's surface and keep walking until gravity pulls me under and I drown. Until my spirit rises through my crown and merges with the energy of the Universe, the essence of nature, the expansive place where my mother has been dancing for the past eight years. I want to be reunited with her, with everything made of ether and invisible fibers. I want to become the ocean, the waves, the moonlight, and the sunshine. I don't want to be in this cage of flesh anymore. I don't want to struggle with the violence of being human. I don't want to fight for my integrity, my dignity, or my sanity. I want to go home. I don't belong here.

At some point, my boyfriend stood in the doorway of the closet. We argued about something. I was hot all over and had lost sense of where my body ended and where the world began. The fever dream was back, and this time it was never going to go away.

"I'm leaving," he said.

"Are you breaking up with me?"

"Yeah, I guess," he said.

I faded in and out of consciousness. The heat. The hurt. All of it pressed down on me. I'm not okay. I'm going to kill myself, I thought. It felt like a good idea. It felt like the *best* idea. Like the most courageous thing I could do. Stop fighting. Surrender to whatever it was that had been chasing me for so long.

I found a bottle of Xanax and a bottle of Tylenol PM in the bathroom. I ran out of the house and dashed a few blocks to the beach. I felt sand between my toes and saw stars overhead. My body was wrenched with a dizzying pain that had nowhere to go. Mom was holding my hand. I ate mouthfuls of pills with my eyes squeezed shut. I heard the howling roar of crashing waves followed by silence and a weighted blanket of darkness.

And then I was gone.

"Can you hear me? Do you know where you are?" A voice from the darkness penetrated my sleep.

I heard it but was too disoriented to speak.

"Do you know your name? Do you know what year it is?"

I struggled to open my eyes. I saw blurry people, strangers hovering over me. The fluorescent brightness was too much. My eyes squeezed shut. I drifted away again.

"Gabrielle, you have to eat something. You have to eat, or we are going to put this tube down your throat." The strangers were threatening me.

"Get away from me. Get the fuck away from me," I croaked, my voice hoarse from lack of use. I thrashed about, swinging my arms and kicking my legs. I felt a rush of adrenaline. Super-human power.

They held me down and shoved a thick tube down my throat. I ripped it out. More strangers came. The more they sent, the more I fought. I was a blur of hands and hair and spit. My thin wet gown was tearing off. I was naked from the waist down. The sturdy metallic bed rocked back and forth like a boat in a storm. The needle in the fold of my arm was bleeding.

I screamed at the top of my lungs, "Get the fuck off me! Get these fucking people off me!"

For a second, they stopped. The strangers locked eyes with me. Their mouths hung open. They loosened their grips slightly, their hands now holding instead of clenching.

Then someone said in a soft voice, "Look, you have to eat something or we'll have to restrain you and force you to eat. We know you don't want that. Can you please just eat something?"

I stared without expression. The only way to get them to go away was to give in. Again.

"Please?" the kind voice asked.

I nibbled on the tasteless hospital food. They slowly backed away. I bit. I chewed. I swallowed. My chest rose and fell with heavy breaths. My neck and shoulders were tense. My mind searched for a way to escape. I drifted in and out of consciousness. My mouth felt dry. My head was heavy. My hair stuck to my face. Ugly pastel curtains dangled from metal hooks around me. Someone held a phone to my ear. I heard voices—familiar people wishing me well and sending me love. I might have been dreaming.

They put me in a chair with wheels. They pushed me through white hallways and sliding glass doors into the blinding sun. They put me inside an ambulance. The doors closed. I stared at my bare feet. The van rocked me side to side. The van stopped, and I entered a faceless, nameless building. Cement walls. No windows. A woman sat in a glass box. She talked to me through a hole in the glass. She asked me questions. I stared at her. I didn't respond.

Eventually, I asked, "Where is the phone? I need to use the phone."

Homeless, crazy people were sitting in front of a TV, watching a violent talk show with people throwing fists at each other, people being restrained by big black bodyguards.

The woman didn't let me use the phone. Two people walked me down a hallway. I saw two rooms—one for men, one for women. They each held a dozen beds, with the terrible metal bedframes they'd had in my college dorm. There were no sheets. When I asked why, they said, "You might hurt yourself with them."

There is no more me in me. I am not me, no me. This walking, talking body is not a real person. There is no one in here that I recognize.

I lay down on the plastic mattress.

Maybe I am a ghost. Maybe I died, and this is where you go when you kill yourself.

Someone yelled, "Five-minute break in the yard."

I went to the door. People slouched in a fenced-in yard and smoked cigarettes. The grass was brown and dead. The fence was so tall and thick I couldn't see through it, over it, or past it.

I returned to the plastic bed. I fantasized about death. I screamed at God in my mind. *Why didn't you take me? Why did you refuse me? Why did you spit me back out into the world?*

The sun went down and came up again. The day repeated itself over and over.

Will they leave me in here forever?

I heard a woman's voice. "Gabrielle, you have a visitor."

I didn't move.

"Gabrielle, get up. You have a visitor."

Like a wilted flower, starving and barren, half the size of my original self, I wandered into the lobby.

"He's waiting for you in the office," she said.

I walked through the door just as my father turned and made eye contact with me.

9

THE MEDICAL OFFICE WAS cold, or maybe it was just me. I sat in a stiff chair next to my father across the metal desk from another doctor while they talked about me, the patient. I felt broken beyond repair. I still didn't know where I was or why I was there. The four walls around us were made of cinderblock and there were no windows. I hadn't seen a window in the entire place except for the glass wall at the reception desk. The sense of confinement was absolute. Two men were discussing my future, my fate, and there was nothing I could do about it.

"You're in a holding center for people with nowhere to go. They brought you here from the hospital. I told them to keep you until I arrived," my father informed me.

I didn't respond. It horrified me that I was locked up because of him.

"Are you going to do it again?" he said.

I don't know, I thought.

"No," I said.

"Why were you taking Klonopin?"

He would never understand. I took it because I'm in so much pain that there are no words to describe it.

"I don't know," I said.

"You shouldn't take stuff like that unless you get it from a doctor. Where did you get it?"

"My boyfriend gave it to me."

"Why?"

"To help me sleep on the plane."

He made a face. "That's stupid. You should know better than that."

Shame filled me. I knew he expected me to be the perfect daughter, to fulfill all of his paternal dreams.

"Did you know that one of the side effects of Klonopin is suicidal ideation?" He shoved a medical book in my face and pointed to a black and white paragraph, small text.

Clonazepam, brand name: Klonopin

Sedative used to treat seizures, panic disorder, and anxiety. Controlled substance.

Can cause paranoid or suicidal ideation and impair memory, judgment, and coordination. Combining with other substances, particularly alcohol, can slow breathing and possibly lead to death.

"You can only leave if you promise not to do it again," my father said.

"I promise." I prayed my pledge would be enough for them to release me. Anyplace was better than here. My home had been burglarized. My boyfriend had broken up with me. My life was a mess. But surely, I could call a friend and find a couch to sleep on while I got myself together.

The men stood and shook hands. I followed my father into the hallway. The ache in my gut was so wretched I stood half-bent like an old woman.

"Let's go," he said.

I followed him out of the building into a blazing sun that burned my eyes and skin. My mind was shattered. The world felt intensely cruel and unforgiving.

My father didn't seem to notice my condition, or if he did, he didn't mention it. He drove to a pharmacy where he bought me more drugs. Zoloft, an anti-depressant, and iron supplements, because, he said, my depression was probably caused by anemia.

Imagine that. All this time I thought I was truly fucked up but I just had an iron deficiency.

We walked across the street to a diner where he insisted that I eat something. The diner mocked me with its hot-pink seats and its stunning cheerfulness. I hated it. We ordered food. When it arrived, the smell of it made me gag. In between big sloppy bites of his hamburger, my father told me how he was very busy at home, how he didn't have to come to Miami to rescue me, how it was a gesture of reconciliation like the time we went to that therapist. How he'd tried to make amends with me many times and I was always rejecting him.

The guilt he was serving tasted like vomit in my mouth. I stared at the pancakes in front of me. The brown syrup disappeared, absorbed into the round yellow cakes.

"I know you think I made a lot of mistakes," he said. "You're making your own mistakes now."

A fountain of grief swelled inside me. I wept like a baby, tears streaming down my face.

"Why are you crying?" he asked, genuinely confused.

Sounds were muted. My vision was blurry. I couldn't make it stop. My unhinged mind swung in every direction.

The self-abusive dialogue came rearing back. *I'm a loser. I'm worthless. Everybody else has their shit together. People my age have careers and husbands and wives and houses and 401Ks. I don't even know what a 401K is.*

My father kept chewing, at a loss about what to do with me.

I knew what he wanted me to say. He wanted me to apologize, to admit that he was right, and I was wrong. To agree to return to Scranton with him, settle down, and be the wife and mother he believed every woman is meant to be. His expectations enveloped me like shackles. There was nothing I wanted less than to be married and pregnant and living in Pennsylvania.

Why did I have to be the person he wanted me to be? He wasn't the father I wanted him to be. He thinks that one trip to Florida and some fucking pancakes make up for his abuse. What the fuck am I doing in this diner with him? Why am I such a coward? What's wrong with me?

The heat of rage replaced the moisture of grief, and I became a humid, sticky mess. Snot ran down my face. My limbs burned.

This is all his fault. I am like this because of him.

I wanted to scream. I wanted to run out of the ridiculous diner waving my arms like a lunatic. I wanted to dart out in front of traffic and get hit by a car. I wanted to throw the pancakes at the wall and smash the dishes into bits.

I did none of those things.

I blew my nose into the napkin, and wiped my face with my sleeve.

Then I apologized to my father for crying and thanked him for coming to Miami to help me.

A few weeks later, during the summer of 2005, I walked through the pitch-black night down the winding streets of the Hollywood hills in Los Angeles. Coyotes howled nearby. I silently filtered into the back door of a warehouse with the others, like an army of white ghosts. I removed my shoes and covered my head. The space was dark except for a few candles on an altar. I found a spot on the floor to roll out my sheepskin mat and settled in for the two-and-a-half hours of sadhana, a spiritual discipline that promised to awaken my soul to its destiny.

The Kundalini Yoga teacher I'd met in Miami the previous year was seated cross-legged at the front of the room in her silk sari and glistening jewels. She was the reason I had driven across the country in my rickety Jeep Wrangler. I had enrolled myself in a nine-month spiritual boot camp to cleanse my sins and purify my soul. I drove as far away from Miami as I could get to start a new life; a better life than the one that had landed me in the hospital.

"Your body is the temple of God, and your soul is the Divine Guru within," the teacher said. "When a person gets up in the morning and does the sadhana, all the angels, all saints, and sages come to listen. Recitation of this prayer will lift you from the deepest depression, insecurity, nightmares, and loss. If in morning sadhana one cannot curtail the barriers and get to oneness, I don't think there is any other time it can happen."

Her words soothed me and made me feel like I had made a respectable decision. A haunting and beautiful kirtan chant filled the space. A chorus of voices sang along. The music moved through me, softening my muscles, and replenishing my hollow heart.

After some time, the teacher told us to put our hands in prayer pose and chant "Ong Namo Guru Dev Namo" three times. The room filled with a buzzing nasal sound that vibrated the walls.

Then she turned up loud music and yelled, "Dance! Dance!"

Startled by her strong orders, I jumped to my feet. I moved quickly and intensely. The people around me were jumping, flinging their bodies, and waving their arms. Whenever we slowed down or lost momentum, she yelled, "Keep up! Keep up!"

After about 15 minutes, I was panting and sweating, terrified of being the one to stop moving. Suddenly, shaking took over my body. The song was dancing *me*. It got stronger and stronger until it penetrated the frozen spots in my neck, shoulders, and back. Tears rolled down my face. I was cracking open, muscles trembling, emotions releasing.

Then we moved into asana practice. The teacher called out her commands. "Flex the spine! Breathe rapidly through the nose! Close your eyes!" The exercises blurred, one into the other.

After about an hour, she told us to lie on our backs on the floor. Then she started playing an enormous brass gong. The reverberation moved through the room. I felt like the cells of my being were being scattered throughout the Universe. I faded into nothingness. I may have dozed off.

Then she whispered, "Inhale..."

We wiggled and stretched and sat up in a cross-legged position. Soft music surrounded me. Her next command was, "Sing." I didn't know the words, but I sang anyway.

> *May the long-time sun shine upon you. May all love surround you. And the pure light within you guide your way home.*

I felt tired and dizzy. I was totally spaced out.

The song finished. There was stillness. Beams of pink sunlight started to stream in through the overhead skylights.

It was a new day.

We had an hour to recover before the next session. I flipped through my Aquarian Teacher textbook as I ate oatmeal and drank Yogi Tea in the vegetarian café. In the daylight, I discovered the space inside this "spiritual village" warehouse was massive and intimidating. In the center of the room was a stage with a huge brass gong, guarded by life-size statues of Indian goddesses. Behind the stage, candles burned on an altar, illuminating pictures of saints and gurus. Sacred paintings adorned the walls and hung from the rafters of the cathedral ceilings.

From my seat at the long wooden communal table, I could see the registration desk. Next to it was a gift shop with books, music, jewelry, clothing, and more. Soft Persian rugs covered the hardwood floors leading to a wellness center on the left and an art gallery on the right. Students were mingling, chatting, and shopping. I wondered if they would like me, if we would get along, and if we would become an actual sangha, a spiritual family, during this training.

The girl next to me introduced herself as Marlene. She had sparkly blue eyes and a big smile. I immediately felt some relief. We swapped stories about our backgrounds and experience. I told her about my doctoral research. She had just finished her Ph.D. in psychology. I shared my passion for massage therapy. She was excited about her work as a counselor at an addiction treatment center. "I'm going to teach them yoga," she said. "I think it will really help them."

"That sounds amazing."

"You should come to check it out sometime."

It felt like her invitation was sincere, and it was comforting to make a like-minded friend. I made a mental note to visit her at the center as soon as possible.

At seven that morning, we gathered at the feet of five Sikh teachers, three men and two women, dressed in traditional white attire with turban cloths wrapped around their heads.

"It took you eight million lifetimes to become a Kundalini Yoga teacher. This is your good karma, your good fortune to be here," one of them said.

Whoa! I thought. That's a long time.

"Each day, live to elevate yourself. Each day, elevate one person. Make elevation your religion, and you shall reach infinity," said another teacher.

Yes! I want to elevate!

"You know how to drive a car, but you do not know how to drive your life. There is only one thing you should know: conquer yourself.

Your job is to discipline yourself. Your job is to control yourself," said another teacher.

I need to conquer myself. Got it.

So many previous paths had not worked. Not modeling. Not Miami. Not even all the therapy had cured me of my self-destructive tendencies. I needed this yoga thing to work. I needed to find whatever secret sauce would keep me on the straight and narrow path to sanity.

I had rented a room a few blocks from the yoga studio, with a breathtaking view of the green hills and the glistening city in the distance. I decorated my room like an Indian temple, thinking it might create some miracles for me. I set up an altar on top of my brass trunk with candles, incense, and a Buddha statue. I printed out images of holy people like Dalai Lama and Yogi Bhajan and hung them on the wall. Maybe with the help of the gurus, I thought, I'll be able to get through this yoga training and finish my dissertation.

I had to cross several hurdles to graduate from my Ph.D. program. First, I had to get through a literature review, which was an analysis of every book about my topic, of which there were many. Then I had to complete interviews with several women healers, transcribe the interviews, and analyze the transcripts for themes. Finally, I had to say something smart and original that had never been said before—in the whole history of humans and language—about the phenomenon of healing and healers. I needed to do all this without having another nervous breakdown.

I was single-focused in my determination because this project—and my mental health - were the only things that mattered to me anymore. None of the nonsense—like being pretty and popular, or being swept off my feet—was meaningful. All the parties and the drama were distractions I didn't need. They only caused me grief. I was determined to keep my head down for the next two years and get my work done. No excuses.

Even so, I was riddled with insecurity and anxiety. Surrounded by hundreds of books and journals and buried in stacks of research, I had zero confidence that I could get it done. Fifty percent of people who attempt a doctoral degree never complete it. I didn't like those odds at all. Not only did I need fortitude, but I also needed a fucking miracle.

I opened "The Heroine's Journey" by Maureen Murdock and read the words on the page:

> Women are healers; we know the mysteries of the body, blood and spirit because they are one and the same. Women are lovers; we joyfully embrace each other, men, children, animals, trees, listening with our hearts to their triumphs and sorrows. Women are alchemists; we uncover the roots of violence, destruction and desecration of the feminine and transform cultural wounds. Women are the protectors of the soul of the earth; we bring the darkness out of hiding and honor the unseen realms. Women are singers, dancers, prophets, and poets; we ... help ourselves remember ... who we are as we journey through life (p 185).

I had truth bumps on my skin and resonance in my heart. This is my purpose, I thought. This work, this story, this message.

I sat for hours reading, writing, and praying—pushing through my messy emotions and insecurities. Little by little, my research unfolded like seedlings pushing up through the soil.

I typed on my laptop:

> They have been called drummers, dreamers, diviners, seers, oracles, psychics, prostitutes, priestesses, prophets, mystics, midwives, rainmakers, skywalkers, shamans, witches, herbalists, curanderas, and medicine women, to name a few

of their titles. They existed in conjunction with Goddess-centered religions that date back thousands of years. They have held positions of power and leadership and healed countless people with their spirit, prophesy, hands, and herbs. Their stories inspire with the message of ambition, intellect, adversity, and triumph. They have been and continue to be a significant thread in the fabric of our world. They are women healers.

It felt like the words were writing themselves. I kept breathing and typing my way through the data from the National Center for Complementary and Alternative Medicine (NCCAM), the philosophies of the scholars that influenced me, the autobiographical literature by women healers, and the examples of healing arts practices.

I defined my new beliefs, a perspective that had been forged in my personal transformative fires during the previous decade of reflection. I contrasted that worldview with the perspective and practices of Western medicine. I didn't hesitate to express my dissatisfaction with how I felt underserved by many allopathic doctors.

Then I dove into the history and lineage of medicine, revealing an orchestrated and thorough campaign to stamp out the woman healer during the Middle Ages. After thousands of years of midwifery and herbology, the patriarchy tortured and executed hundreds of thousands—up to one million—women for the crime of helping other women.

When my wrists cramped and my back ached from sitting at my desk, I took a break and walked through the streets near my house. I passed one multi-million-dollar mansion after another, each more beautiful than the one before. I imagined what it must be like to live in one of those houses, to lounge by the pool all day sipping on vodka, or whatever rich L.A. people did.

One day I found myself standing at the top of the Hollywood hills facing a beautiful blue reservoir. Around the lake's perimeter was a dusty dirt path, and dense brush reminiscent of South Africa. A large bird with a wide wingspan flew overhead. I recalled the Gaia hypothesis, and how it described our planet as a living system. I thought about ecofeminism and the perspective that women are the protective caretakers of the planet. I thought about the healing power of nature and all the times she gave me serenity. Life felt suddenly peaceful and calm. My mind was empty except for the full reflection of the scene before me. All of the worry and doubt and stress and strain were gone. I felt an ease of well-being that spread out like the hills around me. I just had to keep going. Put one foot in front of the other. I was beginning to believe I might be able to do it.

During my next yoga training weekend, we started again at 3:30 am and practiced until the sun came up and went down again. I raised my arms and breathed rapidly in and out of my nose, doing "breath of fire" as the teacher instructed. The speed and force of the air made my body shake. I was vibrating all over. We moved into stretch pose, legs hovering a foot off the ground. More breath of fire. More trembling. Beads of sweat formed on my forehead.

About ten exercises later, the teacher let us rest as she stroked the gong. As I was lying down, I saw a holographic image of my third eye being projected out in front of me from the center of my forehead, crystalline and multicolored like a prism of light. Then I traveled into a three-dimensional model of my DNA, colored balls and all, and saw the structure configuring itself into a new formation.

I was disoriented and weary when the instructor told us to sit up.

After the closing song, I gathered my things and prepared to leave. The teacher pointed at me. "You. Come and see me."

A line of women always looked for her council after class. As I waited in line behind the other students spilling their problems and begging for advice, I wondered if I had done something wrong and was in trouble.

When it was my turn, she asked, "Are you on drugs?"

"What? No!"

"Not even pharmaceuticals?"

"I'm taking an antidepressant medication," I admitted.

"You have to get off it. It's frying your nervous system."

"It is?"

She nodded. "That's why you're shaking in class."

Oh my God, this is so humiliating, I thought.

"Breathe," she commanded. "I want to see you breathe."

I took a shallow breath, mostly chest, no belly.

"You're not breathing properly. You're barely alive."

If only she knew.

"Boil ginger in water. Drink it every day."

"Okay. Um, I have this other problem... um, boils...." The anger festering in my body had transformed into excruciating boils on my legs and ass. If I accidentally bumped one of the boils, waves of pain rushed through my body so strong that I grew dizzy and light-headed.

"The same thing happened to me in my training. You are detoxing. Keep doing the yoga."

"Okay," I mumbled.

Even though it was awkward, this was exactly the kind of advice I wanted. I longed to live without drugs, to heal naturally and completely. I wanted to detox every bad thing that had ever happened to me. I didn't care if I shook or bled the whole time. I needed to be free.

My friend Marlene was waiting for me by the door. She invited me to teach an activity at her addiction center.

I felt nervous about the invitation. I had never been to a drug treatment center, and I'd never officially taught anything before, but I remembered the dorm meetings with the college girls seven years earlier. I was excited to dive in with all the knowledge and experience I had acquired since. Maybe it would be a fun hobby.

Little did I know, this was the beginning of my next career.

10

DRIVING UP THE MALIBU mountains toward the rehab, I felt like I was venturing into the hills of Spain. I followed Marlene's directions, turning down a dirt road to a cluster of luxury cabins in the woods. It was gorgeous.

Marlene waved excitedly from the gravel parking lot. "Welcome to Milestones," she said. She gave me a quick tour of the property. We wandered by a field filled with horses, a circus trapeze, a swimming pool, a dining hall, a high-end fitness studio, meeting rooms, and more.

This is a resort, not a rehab! I thought.

"How much does it cost to stay here?" I asked.

"About $40,000 a month. I work for a place in Newport Beach that charges $90,000 a month," Marlene said. "It's mostly celebrities and rich people." Marlene seemed unfazed by the opulence of it all. "They can afford it."

I had no idea anything like this existed. I followed Marlene into one of the cabins, where we prepared to do an art activity similar to the ones I had learned in my art psychology studies. The space was warm and inviting. Sunbeams cut the room in slices of light. We spread art supplies on a soft blue carpet.

Six people wandered in. They looked drained and annoyed.

Someone needs to light their fire, I thought.

We took turns introducing ourselves, first names only. I studied the others' faces, searching for some sense of who they were and why they were there. I told them how excited I was to be there and explained the art activity while handing out big sheets of paper. I exuded as much passion as possible, hoping that my energy would be contagious. They slid off their chairs and onto the floor. They hunched over their papers, busily scribbling colorful lines like a gang of toddlers. I watched with delight as the drawings took shape. It made me happy to see them so engaged. Marlene grinned at me. I could tell that she was enjoying it, too.

After about twenty minutes, the participants took turns explaining their artwork. Stories spilled forth about untold feelings, adventures, and aspirations. They were animated as they described their pictures. It was amazing to see the increase in energy and enthusiasm. It reminded me of the group sessions I did in college with the dorm girls.

They thanked me for coming and asked when I would be returning.

I was delighted. I wanted to do it again. It was so effortless it didn't even feel like work.

When Marlene walked me out to my car she said, "You're a natural teacher."

I'd never imagined myself as a teacher, but somehow, I knew she was right.

Although the teaching seed was planted, I was still very much a student, and I had a lot of work to do. My dissertation interviews with the women healers were laborious but they offered deep wisdom and insights. I heard stories about healing and transformation, being called to a spiritual path, recovering from illnesses or struggles, connecting

108

with nature, and feeling the universal energy of all living things. I heard a consistent expression of gratitude, appreciation for mentors, difficult lessons, nature, and for life. The women said that they learned about all kinds of things that they never dreamt were possible, and that they continued to be students of life no matter how much they learned.

Mary Jo, my teacher, said her journey was not always easy, but she regarded each obstacle as an important life lesson that helped her become a better healer. She believed that struggles were opportunities to clear up issues so that she could help others get to the roots of healing. She also felt the phases of her life were analogous to the seasons of nature, and that she repeatedly experienced times of death and rebirth. She told me it was really important to have a support system of people who can share your life experiences, your soul experiences, who'll nurture you and help you as you go through the different things that you do.

Jean, a woman who practiced Native American and Peruvian healing, used shamanic journeywork to overcome breast cancer. She said the word "healing" is misleading because all she does is hold a space for people to expand and awaken. She focused on the body because she felt it was the source of all wisdom. For her, healing is a series of cycles, or learning curves, that take us to new levels of awareness. Just like Mary Jo, Jean said there would be plenty of challenges and advised me to plan lots of support if I intended to work in the healing arts.

I learned more about miracles and medicine from Allison, who'd used Shiatsu to heal from pelvic inflammatory disease. She thought that healing came from listening and that people just wanted to be heard and accepted for who they are, not for who we want them to be.

Allison preferred to be called a teacher rather than healer because she gave others the tools they needed to heal themselves.

When she told me about her appreciation for nature and meditation, I recalled praying to the gods of the North, South, East, and

West in the forest with my CIIS classmates. I recalled the chills I felt at hearing the ancient prayer for the first time.

Toward the end of the conversation, Allison repeated the same information about life cycles that Mary Jo and Jean had described. She said that there were many levels of cycles happening throughout her life.

I let out a big sigh of relief. It felt good not to be so alone in my personal evolution. I'd thought I was the only person on the planet who was on such a roller coaster. Now it seemed that it was normal for other women to go through cycles of death and rebirth, falling apart and reaching new levels.

But I was also concerned. I believed them when they said that a support system was important, but I didn't know how to begin assembling one. It would be many more years before I figured it out.

The weeks flew by as I continued researching, interviewing, and writing. I was nearing completion of both my doctoral degree and my yoga teacher training. I was beginning to see similarities between the books that I read about women healers and the stories that the women were telling me.

We were all wounded healers on a journey of learning and self-transformation. Following a calling of the soul, a life mission, and a heroine's journey, we were taking diverse ideas and practices and creating an integral approach to healing. I thought those could be the themes for my dissertation and made a note to watch for more insights about them as I continued my research.

Yoga made me stronger and more confident. The boils healed, and the panic attacks were gone. It had been months since I'd had a nightmare. The process made me think that I could become more open, aware, sensitive, expansive, and conscious if I stayed the course.

I was given a new name by my Kundalini Yoga Instructor, Siri Kirn—pronounced city-kitten—which means "Great Ray of Light." I hoped that someday I would live up to that title.

The final months of working on my dissertation required multiple drafts of a 300-page document going back and forth to my committee. Each gap in citation or research was identified, and each line was groomed for perfect spelling, punctuation, and grammar. I carved out words, phrases, and ideas like a madwoman, while trying to keep my eye on the finish line. I prayed the manuscript would serve others who read it. I crossed my fingers that it would make a small contribution to the massive amount of literature about healing that already existed.

Even though the dissertation was an academic exercise, it felt like each page was telling the story of my soul. The act of writing was so intense and transformative that it changed me a little more each day. I got tears in my eyes when I re-read it before submitting it for the final review.

I was longing for wisdom, drowning in chaos, hoping the women healers would throw me a lifeline—and they delivered. I learned so many things; profound insights that pierced me and reverberated in my being. I don't know what I would have done if I did not have their stories to soothe and reassure me; how I would have survived if I had not read the hundreds of memoirs about wise women on the heroine's journey. I don't know how I would have maintained my sanity as a semi-psychic, empathic awakening woman on the wounded healer's journey. Thank Goddess I had the good fortune to learn from the women who came before me.

When I arrived in San Francisco for my dissertation defense, I was giddy with excitement. I entered the downtown building with the banner that said *California Institute of Integral Studies*. I was dressed in a flowing hippie skirt, gold sandals, and a colorful scarf wrapped around my head.

Once I was seated in the conference room with my committee they asked me, "What was your experience of doing the dissertation?"

"This was the hardest thing I've ever done in my life," I admitted.

"If you had to sum up the entire experience in one sentence, what would it be?"

I took a long pause and eventually answered, "I value myself more as a person for having done this project." It was so true. I'd achieved a goal that I hadn't thought I could reach.

"Congratulations, Dr. Pelicci, your dissertation has been approved," the committee chair announced.

Leaving the building that day felt more like a beginning than an ending. I was shocked that I had completed the project that I thought would never end. I was "approved" in the eyes of the professors who I held in such high regard.

I have arrived! I thought. What next?

If what the women healers had said was true about life being a series of cycles like the seasons, then I felt like the winter decay of Miami had passed and the springtime regeneration in Los Angeles was successful. Now I was ready for the summer harvest.

The idea of teaching was pulsing inside me. I applied for a dozen different professor positions across the country, never expecting any of them to accept me. I was shocked when, on August 6, a few days after my 35th birthday, I received an email from Georgian Court University in New Jersey offering me an adjunct faculty position—if I could be on campus by August 17th for the new student orientation. I had 11 days to pack up my Los Angeles apartment and drive 3000 miles to start my new job.

I'll be there, I emailed in response.

I gave away most of my belongings in a yard sale, including several hundred books, and stuffed the few remaining things into my Jeep. Then I drove across the country as fast as I could.

I was in awe when I arrived at the expansive historical campus, which encompassed more than 150 acres of gardens and walking paths.

The main education building was an old stone casino built in 1899. Within it was an enclosed polo court, swimming pool, ballroom, and bowling alley. The other side of campus offered five athletics fields and an enormous wellness center where I was assigned a state-of-the-art classroom for my course.

Georgian Court University was founded in 1908 by the Sisters of Mercy as a women's liberal arts college. With an inaugural class of seven young women, they set out to offer a quality education rooted in the values of respect, integrity, justice, compassion, and service. Over the next one hundred years, Georgian Court's programs and facilities grew, along with its reputation for graduating scholarly women of the highest caliber.

I had to pinch myself when I settled into my desk.

Is this real? Did I just become a college professor? No freaking way!

More than a decade had passed since I was a college student. Not only did I have a massage license, Healing Touch certification, a yoga certification, and a doctoral degree, I had wisdom in my bones. I could put my hands on people and help them heal. I could make recommendations for exercise, diet, and lifestyle changes. I could speak eloquently and intelligently about physical and mental health. I was a born-again teacher, and I was ready to preach the gospel of well-being.

I pushed the desks and chairs into a circle so we could all see one another. I wanted to create intimacy and safety and a feeling of belonging. I wanted to give these women a place to talk, to tell the truth, to ask questions, and to be unguarded. I wanted us to help and serve each other. I didn't want to be a talking head at a podium or an intimidating speaker on a stage. I wanted them to relate to me, to trust me, and to know that we were all in this together.

When I stood in front of my students for the first time, it felt like the most natural thing in the world. Since it was a graduate program in holistic health, the women's ages ranged from twenty to sixty. I was eager to learn about them—why they chose the program and what they hoped to achieve. As I looked out at the dozen faces staring back at me, I already loved them for being there, for pursuing holistic health, and for trying to make their lives better. These were my people.

During the first class, we went around the room introducing ourselves. I told them a little about my journey from traditional medicine to holistic medicine, leaving out the scary parts like the abuse and suicide attempt. I shared the things I learned from Alternative Medicine and how I was able to heal from many things like migraines and cysts by changing my habits and my mindset. I mentioned my dissertation research and the books about women healers. I was eager to help them discover some of the things that I'd discovered so that they could reduce pain in their lives, enhance their well-being, and have tools in their toolbox to take care of themselves.

As I was talking, I could feel all the pieces clicking into place—how my traumas had led to my healing, which led to my ability to give others self-healing tools; how synchronicity and purpose were manifesting in my own life, just like they had for the women healers I'd interviewed; how I did not set out to pursue a career in medicine like my father and yet here I was, practicing medicine, albeit a different kind, one that empowered the patient instead of the doctor; how I had the great fortune of discovering so many different kinds of methods and tools that could be used for self-care; how I had been mentored and guided by the most amazing people and now I had the privilege of doing the same for others.

The students stared at me with rapt attention. I could tell they were a little nervous to introduce themselves. One by one, they began to speak.

Leslie was a young, beautiful bulimic girl. "My mom is an alcoholic," she said, "and I want to learn how to heal naturally. I want to help my mom, and I want to help myself. I love food. I think we can use food to heal anything."

Beth was a physical therapist with 23 years of experience who wanted to add more holistic practices to her work. "I had my first Reiki session this week, and it was amazing. I was spaced out for like an hour," she said.

Rita was a bubbly retired grandma with a dozen grandkids. She loved gardening and helping people. "And Gabrielle," she said as she finished her introduction, "I don't know if you're single, but I would love to introduce you to my son."

Dorothy worked at the college and was having painful infertility issues. "I know I need to lose some weight," she said. "I just had my third miscarriage, and I don't know if I'll ever be able to have a baby. I really want to have a baby."

Around the room we went, talking about our experiences of the body, illness, disease, and healing. I learned that some of the women were taking care of sick family members. Others had recently lost loved ones and were still grieving. Their stories were universal—ordinary human experiences—but I could feel each one in her uniqueness, and I knew each one had the potential to become a great healer. We were weaving a sacred circle with our words, invisible bonds forming between us. This was what women had been doing for millennia; what the church tried to wipe out with the witch hunts. Our connection was ancient and critical for a future where we all respected each other and found the medicine within.

After introductions, I set up massage tables and guided the students through the energy-balancing sequence I learned in my Healing Touch training.

"Feel your feet firmly planted on the ground. Connect to the energy at the center of the earth. Draw the energy of the earth up through your feet and into your hands," I said. I felt like the conductor of a grand symphony. The students were the instruments; the energy was the music. As they moved their hands over various parts of their partners' bodies, I watched with pride and joy. I was honored to be continuing the healing tradition in my classroom that was passed down to me from generations of women healers.

In a soft voice, I explained, "Energy is part of everything that exists and sustains living beings. We use our hands to move the life force energy to increase health, vitality, and well-being. Healers have been using energy therapies for five thousand years. In the East, it's the basis of Chinese medicine and Ayurvedic medicine. We are using our bodies as the instruments or vessels for the flow of chi or prana. Becoming attuned to the flow of energy in our own bodies will help us to feel the subtleties of energy in the bodies of others.

"When I did my dissertation research, the women healers told me that health was a state of energy flowing freely in the body, and illness was a state of blocked or stuck energy. They also described the way in which energetic vibrations from someone else can be picked up by our bodies and affect our health. If you concentrate, you will be able to see, feel, and sense the energy. Anyone can do it; you don't have to be a psychic or have special abilities. Energy is a universal language that we share with people from many diverse traditions and cultures." I watched the students absorbing my words and gently touching their classmates. The air in the room was thick with concentration, a quiet presence.

After they completed the practice and changed partners, we sat in a circle to share our experiences.

"My hands were tingling!" said Leslie.

"I think my grandmother was here, but that's impossible because she died last year," said Dorothy.

Rita said, "Oh my God! I was so relaxed that I couldn't move at the end."

With each testimonial, my spirits rose. It tickled my heart to listen to their surprise and shock. Ten years ago, I had been the one in disbelief. Now I was holding the space, teaching others that their sensations and visions were valid and important. I deeply appreciated their curiosity, trust, and enthusiasm. It was so simple and easy to share this medicine with them, and so satisfying to give them a practice they could do for free whenever they had pain or stress or wanted to help someone else. We were connecting and reconnecting. I was passing on a gift I had received, and I was grateful to give it.

Once I had settled into my weekly routine of teaching, I was hoping to coast on the feelings of satisfaction for a while. It had been years since I'd had a romantic partner who excited me, and I was feeling a strong longing to fill the void. I had dated a nice filmmaker in L.A. for a while, but he was thousands of miles away and I wasn't interested in a long-distance relationship. I also had a few dates with Rick, the owner of the rehab where Marlene worked, but he was unavailable.

Most women my age seemed to be married or attached. Even though I didn't want marriage, I worried about being a spinster and living on the fringes of society if I did not acquire a mate soon.

I ached for a partner, someone strong enough to mend the cracks in my being *and* broken enough so that I could do the same for him. My imaginary man had to be good-looking, well-traveled, smart, funny, tall, sexy, and a whole bunch of other things that I had seen in romantic comedy films or Disney fiction.

I was convinced that my happiness would remain incomplete without a significant other, like Tom Cruise in *Jerry McGuire* or Elizabeth Gilbert in *Eat, Pray, Love*. Even though I had been through so much drama with past boyfriends, I was blind to the unconscious patterns driving my compulsion. I was not yet conscious enough or secure enough to pick someone healthy. As long as he gave me a lot of attention, I would be content. Or so I thought.

My lust was visceral. I needed to get my fill—and fast.

11

AFTER NEARLY 20 YEARS of flirting, dating, falling in love and breaking up, I was still single. I didn't feel much closer to romantic bliss than I did back when I fantasized about Kevin, my 2nd grade crush. I wanted a partner. I had watched my mother go through post-divorce dating. She ultimately gave up on men altogether about a decade before she died. I also saw how Dad's second wife moved back in with her mother after she split with my dad. She never remarried either. I didn't want to follow in their footsteps. I yearned for the happily-ever-after. I feared failing at marriage. I was terrified of divorce. I couldn't imagine being middle-aged and single. What would people think? I clung to any men that crossed my path while avoiding the intimacy and union of a mature relationship.

Social norms didn't help much. The media advertised an unattainable perfection of unconditional love. Love songs were odes to toxic, "I can't live without you" relationships. I hardly saw any women who were strong, healthy, whole, and still sexy as hell in the eyes of the opposite sex. If anything, it seemed like men wanted women to be helpless and dependent so they could feel powerful and important. If men wanted me to be weak, then I would be alone. And then I'd be depressed and adopt too many cats and lose my fucking mind. It seemed like there was no way to win.

Other than a few wholesome families that I had met over the years, I didn't have any examples of couples being really good to each other, supporting each other, and growing together—things that were important to me. I didn't know any couples who were living my dream life of travel and adventure. I wanted to be a citizen of the world, not just one place, and I wanted to experience it all with someone by my side.

There are no classes on how to find a partner, or how to be one-half of a healthy couple. None of the therapy or other methodologies I had practiced in my 20s and 30s informed me about the strong ties between childhood trauma and the dysfunctional patterns that were showing up in my relationships, from clinging to avoiding to distrusting to having a difficult time with sharing emotions. All of it was pretty predictable, given my history. But I lacked insight as I vacillated between feeling righteous and helpless. The beliefs I inherited were rooted in victim mentality—"Bad things just happen to me, no matter what I do,"—and shame - "I'm broken and unlovable."

Learning and teaching were gradually rewiring my brain with new beliefs about worthiness and value. I felt a million times better than before I started my doctoral work and yoga training. I was having a positive impact on others, and that made me feel good about myself. I hoped some of my new thoughts and habits would also impact my romantic life. Maybe, with enough prayer and practice, I could become the partner I wanted to be and attract someone similar. The Law of Attraction was a popular concept at the time. I watched the movie "The Secret" over and over. It taught that everything we want or need can be satisfied by believing in an outcome, repeatedly thinking about it, and maintaining positive emotional states to "attract" the desired outcome. I wanted to be a master at attracting the man of my dreams.

I applied the same resourcefulness to my man search as I did to everything else in my life. I placed personal ads on the internet. I reached out to a matchmaker. I joined a gym and Meetup groups.

I lived in the Rittenhouse area of Philadelphia, a cute brownstone neighborhood with local cafes and restaurants, a scenic walking path along the river, and plenty of people to meet.

I hung out at the local bars on the weekends. Aquarius, a quaint wine and tapas bar, was a three-block walk from my apartment. A regular weekend crowd gathered there. I was adopted by this sweet group as soon as I moved into town. We were all looking for love, and we commiserated for hours about the struggles of being single.

The first time I saw Eric, he was standing outside of Aquarius next to a big guy smoking a cigarette. He was good-looking. Brown wavy hair. Dark eyes. Well dressed. After introducing himself, he pointed to Aquarius and said, "That's my place."

I could tell by the way he said it that he wanted to impress me. It worked. He asked about my work, and I told him about teaching and massage.

He said, "I hurt my neck. Can I make an appointment?"

A few days later, my hands caressed his caramel-colored body as I worked out the tension in his head, neck, and shoulders. He told me he loved the way I touched him. We talked about travel. Eric reminisced about the summer camp he used to go to in Virginia and shared his dreams of seeing the world. When I told him about the places I'd visited, he was jealous.

After the treatment, Eric wrapped his arms around me and rested his head on my shoulder in a long lingering hug.

I was intoxicated. My mind was racing. I wanted to say, "Hey, I like you. Do you like me? Wanna be boyfriend-girlfriend?" and get the whole thing over with. I was no good at waiting for anything.

But Eric didn't call me the next day. Or the day after that.

I secretly hoped he was "the one," but if he wasn't going to make a move, I had to keep playing the field.

My inbox was full of eligible bachelors responding to my personal ad. I went on a dating spree for months, my optimism waning with each boring conversation or wandering eye. I felt frustrated and impatient. My panic drove me to keep dreaming, keep scheming. It felt like time was running out. Maybe the internet isn't the place to meet someone, I thought. Where do conscious men hang out? When I saw an advertisement for a local Buddhist retreat, a lightbulb popped on in my head. Off I went into the wealthy countryside on the outskirts of Philadelphia to get me a spiritual man.

I arrived at my home for the weekend, an old stone house perched on four acres of rolling green hills covered with fresh-cut grass, Friday afternoon. Colorful Tibetan prayer flags danced between glass porch lights on the patio. Wind chimes tinkled in the breeze, and an assortment of chairs sat near a glass table flanked by potted plants.

After I took my bags up to my bedroom I looked out the window. More people were arriving. I scanned the crowd for eligible bachelors. Later, I gathered with about fifteen people inside the meditation hall where a painting of medicine Buddha hung on the wall and an altar table at the front of the room held water bowls and candles. I studied each person, wondering who they were, where they came from, and why they were there.

One man, Tom, seemed out of place in his baseball hat and shorts, like he belonged at a sporting event rather than a silent Buddhist retreat. I liked him immediately. His casual style seemed both approachable and nonconformist.

The teacher entered the room. He was wearing a red monk robe and was barefoot. His piercing blue eyes were set deep in his face, under a hairless scalp. I got butterflies in my stomach when I saw him. After he sat down, he smiled kindly, wrapped an orange cloak around his body, took off his watch, rested his palms in his lap, and said, "OM is a lovely word."

We sat cross-legged with straight spines. We all chanted together in low hums until the room vibrated like the inside of a drum. I felt the resonance in my chest and head. For a brief moment, I forgot my urgency for romantic love.

The monk said, "Feel the presence of the Buddha."

I sank in. Energy ran down my arms and up through my head.

"The Buddha held up a flower as a teaching. Students became enlightened. That's all you need. One moment. One flower. One breath," the monk said.

A white butterfly hovered and fluttered over the green bushes outside the window. I felt weightless. I was suspended in completion, residing in a place of reverent totality with the universe. I didn't need a boyfriend to be happy. I didn't need enlightenment. I had everything I needed.

Until the bell chimed.

Rinnnnnng. The reverie was broken. All my humanness came rushing back into the empty space. I wanted to eat because I was hungry. I wanted to turn on my cell phone and check for messages from prospective lovers. I want to flirt with Tom, the guy in the baseball hat.

When I reached the buffet of hot, fresh food at dinner, I filled up my plate and ate it too fast. I couldn't help it. I returned for sweet bread and ginger tea.

My companions and I ate in silence. I looked at Tom several times, but couldn't catch his eye. Well, this is not working, I thought. Why do we have to be silent, anyway?

When I finished eating, I walked outside to watch the rising moon. Golden haze draped around the glowing white orb. I sat on the porch swing and rocked slowly forward and back, listening to the crickets sing.

Tom strolled out. "Can I join you?" he asked.

Woo hoo! I was pleasantly surprised. We weren't supposed to be talking, but I liked his energy, and I wanted his company. "Sure," I said.

He sat next to me on the swing at a respectful distance, and we rocked for a long time in silence. An orange-and-white tabby cat crept by.

In the dark, quiet night, I began to confess secrets to him unexpectedly. "When I'm not thinking about my problems I feel joyful, happy, light, and present. When I think about them, I feel annoyed, frustrated, resentful, and depressed. Does that happen to you?" I asked.

"Of course, it does. I've spent the last two years looking at my own reactions, trying to pay attention to my thoughts and to figure out who I really am," he shared.

An easy conversational pause rested between us. The moon reflected off the glass table. The cricket song was steady as a pulse.

"I have an irrational fear that I'm becoming an old hag, that no one will want me, because I'm almost 36 years old and single," I said.

"Sounds like you're looking for love outside of yourself," Tom said. "No one else can give you what you need to give yourself."

I felt the warmth between our bodies, a subtle tingling sensation. Another long pause drifted by.

"I feel like I'm getting closer and closer to myself. I feel fragile and new. I want to be unafraid of who I am. I want to come out of my shell and be me," I said.

"Take time to find out who you truly are without all the labels and underneath all the judgments," Tom replied.

A tiny bug with an iridescent black body crawled on my arm. Two little antennae. Legs too small to see.

"Does it ever make you scared to address new issues—especially big ones? Even after a lifetime of personal growth, I still feel worried about change," I said. "Like I'm not whatever enough to conquer it."

"Of course. It's hard. If it wasn't, we would be done by now."

After a long while, I excused myself to go to bed. I wondered what would become of me and Tom. He had mentioned that he lived in Atlanta. I wasn't looking for a long-distance relationship. Why does this have to be so complicated? I wondered. Why can't the right guy just fall into my lap?

I fell asleep immediately and dreamt of night critters and a dark forest I was too afraid to explore.

When I returned home, I received an invitation to teach in Saybrook University's Mind-Body Medicine graduate program the following semester. The invitation was a confidence booster. Saybrook students attended classes online and residential conferences, similar to the CIIS retreats. The university also partnered with the Center for Mind-Body Medicine (CMBM), an international organization that attracted thousands of doctors, nurses, social workers, and other health professionals from all over the world. CMBM graduates worked with trauma in communities challenged by war, poverty, crime, addiction, and disasters. It was an exciting way to add more travel and more status to my career. I could easily teach for both schools while living in Philadelphia.

After a few months of preparation, I arrived in Washington DC to participate in Saybrook's Spring 2010 orientation as both a student and instructor at the residential conference. I was teaching a Stress-Management course to the graduate students and also taking the CMBM training with the other faculty members.

On the first day, I joined hundreds of people in the massive hotel ballroom. Dr. James Gordon led us through an expressive meditation that used intensive shaking to wake up the body and release stuck tension or emotion. It was a fun activity reminiscent of Kundalini Yoga, but I wondered why the program was so popular.

We divided into our break-out rooms, and I met with my class. I was the youngest instructor by at least a decade, and younger than many of my students, most of whom had decades of professional experience. I was a little nervous at first, but my teaching at GCU was so successful that I was confident that the same energy and experiential activities would create a positive outcome.

I led my students through guided meditation. We sat in a sacred circle and talked about how the practice can balance our physiology and psychology, quiet the stress response, and enhance our mood. I could see aha moments unfold as the participants relaxed into their bodies and quieted their minds.

Then I guided them through an expressive arts activity, creating vision board collages for the future of their mind-body medicine practices. We talked about the importance of building communities and fostering connections, ideas central to my dissertation research. With each conversation and discussion, I felt like we were coming closer into alignment and resonance. I deeply appreciated the curiosity, trust, and enthusiasm expressed by my students. I felt my purposeful path benefited not only me but all the lives that I touched.

Throughout the weekend, I chatted with people who had worked in Kosovo, Israel, Gaza, Haiti, and different parts of the US. We all shared a passion for self-awareness and self-care. After so many years of feeling like an outsider, it was liberating to talk with healthcare professional peers who shared my beliefs and values.

On the last day, Dr. Gordon met with about eight of us Saybrook faculty members in a cozy hotel suite to teach us some facilitation guidelines and a few more trauma techniques.

"Self-disclosure is an essential part of facilitation," he began. "Using appropriate self-disclosure can be very powerful for the group. It's a way to give your group members permission to share in a more open or vulnerable way. It is also a demonstration that this is a safe place to share."

Then he told us about a family situation that was causing significant stress in his own life. He teared up as he shared his story. I was impressed with his vulnerability but also leery about the process. I did not want to disclose any trauma to my peers. This was a new professional opportunity. The last thing I wanted was for them to know my shameful past. I wanted them to think of me as the shiny, happy young professor and nothing else.

We started the session with a few minutes of guided meditation. We were settled and relaxed when Dr. Gordon explained, "The fight, flight, or freeze response is natural for humans and other animals. When animals experience fight or flight, they release their energy and return to normal activities. The difficulty with humans is that we get stuck in a persistent state of fight or flight, which eventually damages the body. After experiencing trauma, we may get chronic overactive stress response, which is related to decreased immune functioning, anxiety and depression, and other diseases. The good news is, this cycle of chronic stress can be broken with tools like meditation and the other self-care practices we're learning."

Some of the participants around me wore expressions that indicated they'd never heard of this before. I felt frustrated. I'd gotten similar content in my Psychology 101 course in college. Was I going to learn anything new in this program? I felt my attention drifting off.

We connected to biofeedback devices and practiced various breathing techniques to adjust our heart rates. Though the activity and the biofeedback were interesting, it wasn't mind-blowing.

Dr. Gordon must have been reading my mind because he said, "How do you deal with someone who voices their skepticism to mind-body medicine, or to a particular skill? Your challenge is to let people be where they are. Not everyone will like everything we do. That's the beauty of these groups. You can pick and choose the skills you relate to the most, and that work best for your unique experience."

Then Dr. Gordon presented something I had never heard of before: a genogram. He gave each of us a piece of blank paper and asked us to fold it in half, from top to bottom, and then in half again. Next, we opened the paper, which was divided into four sections. Dr. Gordon asked us to put our grandparents in the top section, parents and their siblings in the second section, siblings, spouses, or partners in the third section, and our children, nieces, and nephews in the bottom section.

I froze in horror. *Oh, hell no. There's no way I'm talking about my family in this group. This is a can of worms I will not open.*

Dr. Gordon continued with the instructions. "Join two people in a relationship with a line—solid for marriage, dotted for living together. Slashes can be used to indicate separation, and double slashes indicate divorce. A second or third marriage or relationship can be added along the same line. Each line down from a partnership line represents a child, with the children arranged from left to right from oldest to youngest."

No, no, and no. I am not writing down the names of Dad's multiple wives and his seven children. Not going to happen.

Dr. Gordon said, "Next, add information that describes the nature of your relationships, from close to distant or conflicted. Include information to highlight family patterns, challenges, and strengths."

How do I get out of here? Heat and pressure began to rise in my body, the fateful fever returning.

Dr. Gordon tried to make the activity sound poetic. "A genogram is more than genealogy or a family tree. It is a unique living portrait of your life that can be explored multiple times. It will deepen your self-awareness by discovering the challenges and strengths that link you to previous and future generations. It will give you new perspective and wisdom about your family story."

He actually thinks this is a good idea. Why is everyone filling out their paper? Why do they look so relaxed? I'm not doing this. As the thoughts raced through my mind I went into full fight-or-flight, all-the-emotions-exploding-in-my-brain mode. I was the trauma in the room.

Five minutes passed. I was paralyzed. Ten minutes went by.

"Five more minutes," Dr. Gordon said. I had nothing on my paper. My peers wrote dissertations and created Picasso paintings on the page.

"Ok. Time's up," Dr. Gordon said.

People put down their pencils and studied their pages with pride. Sweat dripped down my arms and underneath my breasts. Even the backs of my knees were wet.

One by one, Dr. Gordon motioned for each person to describe their genogram. I was astonished at all the kind and complimentary things that my peers had to say about their parents and grandparents.

"My dad was my best friend," said David.

"My grandmother was my inspiration," said Ali.

Dr. Gordon's gaze fell on me. I couldn't make eye contact. My throat was in a clamp, and my head was dizzy.

"I...uh...don't do family," I said.

Dr. Gordon frowned. "What do you mean, you don't do family?"

"I don't have family. I have some family, but I don't participate." The room began to spin. My stomach contracted and I feared I might vomit.

"Would you be willing to say more about that?" he asked.

"My mom is dead...I'm estranged from my father. I..."

The rupture came up from my gut, into my chest, and out of my face. I had a full-blown panic attack in less than ten seconds.

"How is your body feeling?" Dr. Gordon asked softly.

I was hyperventilating so badly I couldn't answer. I felt mortified. Humiliated.

"Is there anything you need right now?"

I tried to stand and steady myself. The others in the room blurred into one giant face of concern.

"Would it be okay if we all took a minute to breathe together?" Dr. Gordon asked.

I walked toward the door, but I was no longer in my body. "Excuse me," I managed to say as I opened the door and moved from the room.

Somehow, I made it to the hallway bathroom, where I doubled over in heated sobs of pain.

Motherfucker. Goddammit. Jesus Christ. I raged at myself. At Dr. Gordan. At my father and the fucked-up world I was living in. I thought about how Mary Jo had said that I needed to forgive and heal the relationship with my father because it was holding me back.

Fuck that.

I felt defeated. Crushed. I didn't have time for this. And I didn't want to deal with it. I finally had a career that I loved. I didn't want to stop and deal with my past. I'd wasted enough time on it. I wanted to focus on the future.

I forced my fight-or-flight response to dissipate and put a smile on my face like I had learned to do in modeling.

Happy future. Happy life. Happy future. Happy life. I repeated the mantra as I made my way back to the suite to apologize for my inappropriate behavior.

I escaped the Saybrook conference without much fuss about my outburst. It never occurred to me to trust my peers or Dr. Gordon with my trauma story. No one knew my whole story. Bits and pieces had spilled out in therapy sessions, massage treatments, writing classes, and so on, but no one knew the full extent of abuse, violence, or pain that was my personal history. I held it close to my chest because I felt it diminished me, and made me appear less capable, desirable, impressive, or valuable. Authenticity was attractive in theory, and I could share some details about my physical and mental health struggles, but revealing the graveyard of skeletons, the dirty laundry, and the shameful ugliness of it all, wasn't an option.

And I hadn't the faintest clue how it was affecting my pursuit of romance, or how it would impact my next relationship with Karl, who swept me off my feet.

12

MY WANDERLUST WAS BACK and I wanted to spend the summer in Europe, visiting places that I had not seen on my previous trip. I joined a website called Couchsurfing, an online community that offered free places to stay across the globe. A local Couchsurfing gathering was happening on a Saturday morning in my neighborhood, so I decided to go meet some fellow Couchsurfers, hoping they'd have some good tips for me.

As I rode my bike across town, I passed through Rittenhouse Park with its shady lawn and serene fountains. It was the perfect time of year, not too hot or cold. Couples were strolling around hand in hand, and friends gathered on blankets. For such a big city, Philly always felt like a small town to me.

I arrived at a quaint brownstone building and knocked on the door. Barry, the host of the Meetup, invited me inside, where about 20 people were settling into couches and chairs. It was a humble apartment with lots of light. There were many shelves of books and plants, which made me feel right at home.

The group was a mixed crowd of international people from several different countries. Barry invited us to introduce ourselves one by one, so we quickly got to know each other and build rapport. Seated across from me was a nerdy-looking German guy named Karl. I was curious about him. He had a Ph.D., and he was doing a post-doc in Philly. He made everyone laugh with his thick accent and strange jokes.

We had a lively conversation for a couple of hours. Time flew by so fast that I was disappointed when Barry announced the end of the meeting and kindly hinted for us to go. I hung around on the sidewalk for a few minutes, talking to a girl from South America.

Just as I was about to leave, Karl approached and asked if I wanted to join him at a barbecue. I was definitely in the mood to meet more people and have more conversation. We rode our bikes to South Philly, past fish markets and cheesesteak stands, and made our way to a loft building. We climbed the stairs to the roof where a dozen people were grilling, eating, drinking, and having a good time. When the crowd saw Karl, they cheered. Girls gave him affectionate hugs and guys gave him high-fives and pats on the back. I was surprised by how much attention he was getting. Maybe there's something special about him, I thought.

We were mingling and talking when one guy asked, "Where'd he find you?"

This caught me off-guard. "What do you mean? We met at a Couchsurfing thing this afternoon."

He laughed. "Karl has a talent for catching every beautiful woman in the city."

I didn't feel any chemistry with Karl, but I wondered why he was getting all the women. Was there more to him than met the eye?

When the sun went down, I was chilly and tired. I wanted to go home.

"Let me go with you," Karl said. "Just to be safe."

He escorted me home and stood next to me as I opened the door. He was talking nonstop. "You are very happy and positive and enjoy life. Like me!" he said.

"Thanks."

"I would love to spend time with you. You already did a lot for me."

"Okay."

I opened the door and he followed me inside like a stray animal. It happened so fast I didn't know what to say.

"I...uh, I'm tired," I said, hoping he'd get the hint.

"It's okay. No problem. We can just stay together and rest. I will not be touchy and feely."

I laughed. Karl seemed crazy but charming. I changed my clothes and got into bed. Karl laid down next to me awkwardly. We were barely touching. I still wasn't feeling attracted to him.

"You okay? Your heart is beating really fast." I could feel it thumping along next to me.

"It's a good thing."

We talked for a long time. He told me how much he appreciated that the sky over Philly was blue so many days of the year. He loved riding his bike to work, even in the winter. His favorite thing about the US was the people.

"They are so welcoming and open. Americans seem to be extreme in all ways, and being different is not a problem. Everybody can find their tribe." He told me that he was returning to Germany in two weeks and would be leaving a piece of his heart behind.

When Karl left the next morning, I thought we were parting for good. But he texted repeatedly. He wanted to see me again. He was having a going-away party, and he wanted me to come. Karl's post-doc time at the University of Pennsylvania was over and he had accepted a consulting job in Berlin. He wanted to say goodbye to everyone before he left. I assumed that he had made a dozen friends or so.

When I got to Karl's apartment a few days later, I was shocked to see a mob of people wearing costumes and wigs, wildly dancing and having a blast. It was unlike any party I had ever been at before. The crowd was mostly foreigners, and super friendly. Everyone wanted to know who I was, where I was from, where I had traveled, and where I was going next. I felt an awkward curiosity. Karl gave me a blue wig and insisted that I wear it. I felt weird, but figured, when in Rome...

The festivities lasted all night. When I tried to leave, Karl insisted I stay. After the guests left, we cuddled in his bed. He told me, "You are tickling my brain and inspiring me." His quirky, shameless flirting was growing on me.

After about a week of constant contact and increasing chemistry between us, Karl finally made a move. We were standing on the stairs inside his apartment when he kissed me. It was like lightning, releasing high-voltage electricity between us. His desire for me was intoxicating. We practically tumbled down the stairs lip-locked, groping and undressing each other. He carried me into his room and ravished me. Bent me, twisted me, tossed me around like a rag doll. It was heaven. The bed rattled beneath us and the headboard slammed into the wall. The high that I felt with him was addictive. I was drunk on pleasure.

This one encounter made me feel less alone, closer to reaching my goal of securing a relationship. I didn't really consider whether or not he was a partner I wanted, because I didn't know what my needs were. I was taught that the man chooses you, not the other way around. And I felt chosen.

We spent the next seven days and nights together before Karl left for Germany. We couldn't keep our hands off each other.

Karl knew I had plans to visit Spain in two months. "Come to Berlin! You can teach remotely from there and learn German!" he urged.

"Maybe," I said. "Let me think about it." I was so exhausted I couldn't think straight. Germany wasn't even on my bucket list.

Karl and I exchanged long emails, and longer Skype calls, nearly every day leading up to my departure to Europe. He detailed all of his previous relationships, his experience of women, his dreams of a life partner. He told me amazing stories about what it was like to grow up in his family, about his parents playing music at home, and his dad being silly while his mom rolled her eyes. Could I really have a love like that? Could I really have a happy family? I wondered. It seemed too good to be true.

Two months later, I touched down in Spain and checked into my hostel. I had agreed to visit Germany, but only after I saw the basilicas and beaches of Barcelona. I wandered through the gothic streets, listening to street performers and eating tapas. I lingered in Gaudi's surrealist park, running my fingers along the colorful tiles of the winding staircases. I chatted with other travelers and felt inspired and energized by the conversations and scenic views.

After a few weeks, I boarded a flight to Berlin. The tension that had dissipated in the delightful Mediterranean city returned to my neck, back and shoulders. It felt like a big risk to stay with Karl in Berlin. We hardly knew each other.

When he picked me up at the airport, we embraced like we had been separated for a lifetime. I felt warm and safe in his arms. Maybe everything will be okay, I thought. Maybe he's the one.

It was around 10 pm when we arrived at the building where Karl was crashing with his friend Ani while he waited to move into his new apartment. Before my bag hit the floor, a hysterical Italian woman stormed into the place. She was yelling in half-Italian, half-English, something about how she was in love with Karl, and that he'd led her on with the kissing and holding hands in the park.

I picked up my bag and ran as fast as I could out onto the desolate street. Karl came running after me and Ani followed him. The three of us darted through the neighborhood. I approached every stranger I passed asking, "Is there a hotel nearby?"

Karl was yelling, "Stop, please stop!"

No one spoke English. They had no idea what I was saying. Ani was crying. Finally, I went into a bar and sat on a stool. About one hundred Turkish guys were watching a football game and yelling at the big screen TV. Karl sat down to my right. Ani took the seat to my left.

Several hours and beers later, the whole picture was clear. Karl and Ani were friends. There was hand holding. A kiss. She fell in love. He did not. He'd told her I was coming. She'd said it was okay.

It was not okay.

Karl asked me what I wanted. He tried to find me a hotel room, but nothing was available at two in the morning.

Karl and I went back to the apartment alone, and Ani agreed to stay away.

I had planned on staying with Karl for two months. *What was I going to do now?*

I couldn't express my feelings because I had never done that before. I felt as unsafe as I did when I was a child. I couldn't enforce my boundaries because no one had shown me how. My parents had taught me how to repress and suppress, and to never speak the truth. I was repeating an all-too-familiar pattern of an unfulfilling romance again, but I didn't know to change it. I felt exhausted and defeated. My burning desire for a mate meant that I had to brush this incident under the rug or walk away. I didn't know how to decide.

The next day I got on a train and went to Muenster to stay with a friend I had met in Miami. I crashed on her couch and relayed the whole debacle. Karl called and texted incessantly. He was sorry. It was a mistake. Ani sent me emails telling me that it was all her fault.

"What should I do?" I asked my friend.

"He seems really sorry," she said. "Can you give him another chance?"

A week later, I hesitantly returned to Berlin. I don't do open relationships, I explained to Karl. I only do monogamy.

"I love to see you, hold you, make you laugh, dance with you, and have badass sex with you," he said as he kissed me.

I felt incomplete without a partner, empty without intimacy. Plus, the sex was really good. I convinced myself to try again.

Karl and I picked up where'd we left off in Philly. It was easy to be with him. He was youthful, frisky, and worldly; he was a pretty good match to my Disney version of the perfect guy. We had a rom-com situation and a shared passion for international adventures. I tried to enjoy the moment and not to think too much about the future.

I slowly sank into Berlin, but it was a bumpy ride. German rules were posted everywhere, and I had no idea what they meant. If I rode my bike on the sidewalk instead of the bike path, I got stopped by the police. Garbage cans came in five colors. If I put glass in the blue one or paper in the yellow one, someone would give me a dirty look or stern warning.

Karl worked during the week so I explored the city solo. On weekends, we spent long afternoons in the parks drinking beer and playing music with his friends. It was cool to be grungy in Berlin; messy hair and clothes downplayed status and income. That was not my style. I liked getting dressed up for dinner and drinks, having sarcastic banter, and dancing in a crowded bar. Immodesty also confused and startled me. I was shocked to see Karl's male friends undress in front of me at the pool or lie around naked at the lake. I was prudish in comparison. I had only seen men naked in the bedroom.

When Karl took me to meet his parents, I was hoping to slide right into their storybook family, but they looked at me like a strange piece of furniture that he had imported from America. They were grey and subdued. I was loud and colorful. I didn't understand German etiquette, and they didn't speak a word of English. Little by little, I realized how many cultural differences separated me from their world.

I tried to dress-down my clothes, tone down my voice. I tried to squeeze myself into their box so they would love and accept me just like I'd tried to do with Chris's family ten years earlier. It wasn't working.

When the two months were up at the end of summer, I needed to decide whether to stay or go. Karl and I were mostly happy. I felt the lingering fears about being alone, of ending up like my mother or stepmother. I didn't want to leave without giving the relationship my full effort.

I contacted my supervisor at GCU and asked if I could teach remotely. She gave me the green light. I had work, a place to live, and a partner. I agreed to spend the rest of the year in Germany.

Karl was elated. "Ish libe dish," he said. *I love you.*

I wasn't sure if I was in love or just lust, but I said it back to him, nonetheless.

We settled into a new apartment, filled it with Ikea furniture, and tried to be a domestic couple. I made smoothies in the blender. He played German rap on the stereo. I joined a local yoga studio and made a bunch of English-speaking friends. We ate sausage at the beer garden. He invited friends over for parties that lasted until sunrise.

When winter came, it was dark and cold twenty-four hours a day. Dull sunlight glimmered for about four hours in the afternoon. Rain was bitter, and snow burned cold. Each day felt more confining than the next. I felt like a wilting plant that had lost the will to live.

The best thing about Berlin was the cheap flights to all the major European cities. I booked weekly trips to every destination on my bucket list. I rode a pink Vespa on Roman roads. I ate crepes in a Parisian café. I prayed in the Blue Mosque in Turkey. Each holiday was a welcome reprieve from the winter blues.

Before I knew it, spring arrived, and the ground started to thaw. Karl often traveled for work, and I found a group of expat American women to hang out with in Berlin. We met for lengthy brunches and drank mimosas until we were wobbly. We commiserated about our discomfort with the garbage cans and grungy outfits, the guttural language, and uptight authorities, and laughed at our foibles.

One girl, Wendy, had spent three years in Berlin, trying to adapt to her boyfriend's life. She was worn out to the point of tears. "I can't do it anymore," she said. "I just want to go home."

I empathized with her suffering. It was not easy to change everything about your life to please someone else. I wondered how long I'd last.

I doubled down my efforts to fit in. Nothing felt quite right. I took language classes and tried to converse with Karl's family and friends in broken German. But I felt like a character in a movie, playing a part meant for someone else. I drank Riesling to excess, trying to numb my discontent. Feeling numb was better than facing all the feelings that would come to the surface if I sat in sober solitude for a few minutes. There was too much buried inside of me to be honest with myself.

In the summer, I took another trip to France. I was wandering around the marina in Marseille when something magical happened. I fell madly in love—with a boat. I had always loved sailing. I thought sailboats were a mysterious feat of engineering and beauty. I stumbled onto the Audi Med Cup, an international regatta, took one look at the racing yachts and nearly fainted. They were the fastest, sexiest, most wonderful things I had ever seen.

I hung out every day, flirting and begging my way onto the Mediterranean racecourse. I learned the names of all the boats and crew. I got invited to dinners and parties.

For the next couple of months, I followed the boats to Sardinia and Barcelona. Each competitive performance was more amazing than the next. The sailors introduced me to other races—the 52 Super Series, The Rolex Cup, The Kings Cup. I went to those events, too. My enthusiasm culminated in a job offer to work for the Miami stopover of the Volvo Ocean Race.

Karl was worried. He was hoping I would settle in Berlin, but nothing could keep me away from the boats. They were my refuge and my joy. I began to care more about my happiness than I cared about pleasing Karl. I moved back to Miami and bought a thirty-four-foot sailboat.

Karl and I maintained a long-distance relationship. In the first few weeks, I missed him more than I expected. I had grown attached to his attention and affection. But Florida was also a breath of fresh air. It was refreshing to be on familiar ground. I could finally relax into a city and culture that was natural to me. I worked twenty-four hours a day to help transform Bicentennial Park into a sailing stopover village.

Karl came to visit, and we talked about the future. "I think if we manage to stay so free, not take away the other person's freedom and stay so mentally and physically attracted to each other, then I see very good times coming," he said.

I hoped so. I just couldn't imagine spending the rest of my life in Germany, and a long-distance relationship seemed less than ideal. I didn't want to think about it. I had much more exciting things to focus on.

The sailing village was fantastic. We filled twenty-one acres with seventeen pavilions, exhibits, interactive games, and rides. We had live bands and DJs, jugglers, Miami Heat and Miami Marlins Dancers, beach volleyball, junkanoo bands, high school marching bands, school kids by the busload, the Great Steamboat Race, and all six Volvo Open 70s at our docks. I was in charge of the Customs paperwork and got to ride out on the security boat that met the yachts as they arrived in Miami. It was the best day of my life.

When the festivities died down and my work was done, I returned to Berlin and Karl. The contrast between America and Germany was more depressing than ever. My expat friends and I complained about the same things that we'd complained about the year before. I drank more mimosas and more Riesling and tried not to wonder if this was what I'd be doing for the rest of my life.

One afternoon when Karl was in the shower, a message appeared on his phone from Tatiana. "Mi amor, wir sehen uns am Dienstagabend!" *See you on Tuesday night.* Tatiana was his tango dance partner. They took classes together on Tuesdays.

"I think she's in love with you," I said.

"That's ridiculous," Karl said.

On some of his out-of-town trips he stayed with former female classmates, even when I told him that I expected him to stay in the hotel accommodations provided by his job.

The tipping point came when he spent the day at a "wellness" brothel with his Greek friend. "I just sat in the jacuzzi and laughed with the girls," he said. "I didn't even want to have sex with them."

Arguing about his indiscretions did nothing to change them. He would gaslight me and tell me that I was insecure and jealous. The conflict was so debilitating it made me sick to my stomach. Unable to admit defeat, worried I would never be able to make a relationship work, I just kept denying and trying to adapt.

I was sitting in a café with Karl when my brother Skyped me. When I picked up the call, Joseph looked serious but calm.

"I need to tell you something," he said. "Dad has cancer."

I felt the blood drain from my face. My vision went blurry. My father is going to die, I thought. I have to go home.

Karl didn't know what to say. He drove me to the airport in silence. I was shaking and crying when we got to the gate.

"Maybe you can come back when it's done," he said.

I thought about it. From the moment I had arrived in Germany there had been so many red flags. From the outburst with Ani to the awkward visits with his family, to the debilitating winters and the text messages with Tatiana. I had ignored my intuition over and over again, choosing instead to contort myself into someone I wasn't meant to be. The shame of another failed relationship shook me to my core. This was supposed to be my happily ever after. Now I was single again. After all the effort, I was right back where I'd started two years ago. I felt so much rage and grief, I couldn't speak. Worst of all, I still didn't know why it was happening, or how to make it better.

I gave Karl a cold stare that said, "I'm not coming back." And then I boarded the plane.

Romance would have to be put on hold. I had another funeral to plan.

13

WHEN I ARRIVED AT my father's house in the summer of 2013, I wanted nothing more than to forgive and forget. I wanted to be the good daughter, the compassionate human being. I wanted to rise above the fray, avoid conflict and confrontation, be the better person.

I've always wanted to be one of those people who could let the past be the past. I envy those people. I kind of hate them, too. Injuries and injustice have an ever-present place in my mind. It's not that I think about them all the time, but I'm easily reminded and triggered into feeling the unwanted feelings again. I'm not a resentful person, but I carry the pain, especially when there have been no reparations or reconciliation. I am the kind of person who picks at the scab over and over until the blood tells a story, and everyone can see my wound. I don't like this about myself. I would much rather be quiet, accommodating, and oblivious.

Everything I had learned from Catholicism to Buddhism to my yoga training encouraged me to be virtuous and calm. But my body didn't get the message. I trembled and shook as I drove up the mile-long driveway to Dad's estate, a massive 12,000 sq. ft. stone mansion on 100 acres of land in the countryside near Scranton. There was a 4-car garage, an indoor pool, wraparound balconies overlooking a pond, and brass animal statues scattered throughout the property. To me it seemed pretentious and flamboyant.

My mind burst into chaos at the sight of it:

I don't want to be here.

You have to go.

I feel like shit.

Suck it up.

My father greeted me at the door, gave me an awkward half-hug, and shuffled into the opulent house. I followed behind, feeling like a vagabond checking into a luxury hotel. He gave me a tour of his home, naming the price of each object. "This table was $15,000. These books are original copies, over $1,000 each." He was trying to communicate the value of his life in some way, but I didn't get it.

He didn't look sick or terminally ill. He still had thick black hair and his 1980s mustache. I wondered what it felt like to be dying of cancer. Could he feel it?

His three teenaged sons lined up in the living room. They proudly showed me pictures of a boar they killed on a recent hunting trip. Deer head trophies hung on their bedroom walls. My father seemed proud that they were growing into real men, not "pussies."

My father motioned for me to sit with him at the kitchen table. His wife, Ann, who kept her head down and wouldn't make eye contact, scurried around the kitchen making dinner and cleaning up after kids and dogs and cats.

My father asked me interview questions about my life. "Where do you work? How much do you make? What is your plan for marriage and children?"

Even though I was nearly forty years old, an accomplished professor, world traveler, and former fashion model, I felt like a worthless child in his house. I didn't have the status, salary, or family he expected me to have. My accomplishments didn't count to him.

My throat burned as I forced myself to answer calmly and politely. I told him about some of my European adventures and the classes I was teaching. He seemed pensive, like a doctor listening to my symptoms in an examination room.

When I stopped talking, he said, "You know, it's not too late to go to medical school."

Thick, dense energy swirled around my body, blocked my mind. I stared dumbfounded at the floor.

He walked over to the bookcase and picked up a framed photo of the two of us from the summer of 1977. "This is my favorite picture," he said. We were at the beach, and he was squeezing me tight. We were both laughing out loud, Daddy with his dark good looks, and I with my tiny teeth and moo-cow eyes. It was the last good summer, the summer before I turned three. The summer before he punched Mom in front of me for the first time, the summer before the burn replaced the immense, euphoric love I felt for him.

He stood still for a long minute. Then he said, "They say that if you don't have your health, you don't have anything. It's true. I thought there were more important things, but now I know."

I stood there with no idea what to say.

"I thought I would retire," he went on. "I thought there was more time. I thought we would travel. We had plans to see the world."

If he were my student, I would take his hand and talk to him about all the things he could do to make the most of the time he had left. If he were my client, I would hover my hands above his body or glide them along his skin to soothe his grief and ease his misery. If he were a friend, I would hug him and beg him to tell me what I could do.

I held my breath and squeezed the trembling downward into my gut. He put the picture back on the shelf, shuffled into his bedroom, and closed the door.

I hastened upstairs and into the bathroom. I looked at myself in the mirror. My eyes were vacant, with dark half-moon shadows underneath. A choking sob gripped my throat. I tried to swallow it down. My insides were a volcanic eruption of acid and pain. Tears came hard and fast. I held my breath.

Fuck. Fuck. Fuck.

More shaking and crying. I doubled over and threw up in the sink. Chills climbed my spine and across the back of my neck. I dropped to the floor and curled into a ball, arms tingling, hips aching, forehead pressed against the cold tile. My body and mind were a storm of madness.

My father hadn't told me when he received his esophageal cancer diagnosis. He didn't tell me when it spread to his liver.

My chest tightened. I gagged.

My father had waited until the cancer found its way to his brain. He had only a few months left to live. What was I supposed to do?

I crawled to my knees, then to my feet. I splashed cold water on my face and cleaned up the mess.

I looked in the mirror again. My eyes were big and wide and red.

Some deep part of me said, *I want to hold him accountable for the abuse, for terrorizing me and everyone else. I want him to know he gave me nightmares and panic attacks and ulcers and migraines. He needs to know it's his fault that I don't trust anyone, that I don't feel safe in the world.*

I steadied myself on my feet.

Another part of me said, *Nobody cares about your drama. Nobody likes a complainer. Get over it.*

I was not going to fight with my father on his deathbed. I would never be able to take it back. There would be no confrontation. No redemption. I would do what I always did. I would submit.

I curled the corners of my mouth into a smile like I had learned to do in beauty pageants.

That's better, the second voice said. *Now go back downstairs and help your stepmother with dinner.*

The remaining hours and days of my weeklong visit were a blur. I followed my brothers around the house while they swam in the pool, watched movies, and exercised in the basement. We didn't talk about what was happening. We didn't talk much at all. Every couple of hours, I retreated to shake and cry in the bathroom and then returned with an optimistic grin.

When I was leaving, my father said, "I'm so thankful that we have the chance to be closer. I'm glad you're back in my life. Better late than never."

"Your smiles and laughter in the face of your illness are inspiring. Thanks for being a great role model," I replied.

It was the most pathetic performance of my life.

I flew back to my boat in Miami, which was now my permanent residence. No one knew my father was dying, or how I felt about it. My international travels had left me mostly estranged from my friends in the US, and I probably wouldn't have told them the truth even if we were in touch. "Better not to burden them," was my motto. Radical self-reliance was my mission. I had not yet embraced the importance of support which was central to my dissertation research.

Faced with the prospect of being stuck with my messy feelings indefinitely, I signed up for a week-long meditation retreat so I could regain my balance and restore my sanity.

Michael, a former investment banker-turned-Buddhist monk-turned-suburban retreat owner, owned a rural ranch an hour from the city. His property included a humble house surrounded by farm fields filled with lazy cows and a small lake, which was covered with a buzz of mosquitoes and dragonflies. There were old oak trees and walking paths meandering in different directions. Inside the house were a few simple bedrooms, a kitchen, and a meditation sanctuary where the living room was supposed to be.

I breathed a sigh of relief when I arrived. The place made me feel safe. It was exactly what I needed.

I sat on a firm cushion, surrounded by a dozen strangers, while Michael guided us through a short meditation. Then he gave a teaching on emptiness. He drew a stick figure on a big white easel pad and asked us to think of a difficult person in our life.

"What does this person look like?" he asked.

I thought of my father in his medical scrubs and flip-flops.

The crowd called out adjectives like tall, sloppy, uptight, sick. Michael wrote the words on the pad.

Then he asked, "What does this person sound like?"

I thought of my father's interrogations and criticisms about my life.

We continued through the senses and even picked an animal that best represented the person. Then Michael began asking us to define the senses of sight, sound, touch and so on. Sight is just light reflecting of objects and sound is just waves in the air. We knew where he was leading us.

"So, is it true that brash is a sound out there somewhere?"

"I know what loud sounds like," someone said.

"Do you?" Michael pushed. "Do you think there's somebody out there, somewhere separate from your mind, who is inherently loud? You're wrong. It's time to wake up."

Michael continued the exercise, through every last sensation. With each example, I felt more regret about my projections, my judgments, my unfair conclusions.

It's all me. I am an ungrateful, entitled, selfish, hateful, ugly person. I should be better than this. I should be more compassionate and forgiving. I should control my thoughts and stop smearing the "empty" world with my stupid, self-defeating shit.

I was overwhelmed with grief. Tears streamed down my face. Michael looked into my eyes. I was disgusted and disappointed with myself, but I couldn't look away. I didn't want to hide from the truth. I wanted to pick the scab, to show my wound, to find some balm or some penance, anything to make it better.

After the session, Michael came up to me in the kitchen. "Is everything okay?"

I felt raw and exposed. "That was really painful. I saw all the ways that I'm blaming the world for my suffering."

"Good. Then stop doing it."

Michael seemed stronger than I, the kind of person who could accept, adapt, and move on. I felt weak and powerless in comparison. I wanted to stop the pain. I wanted to control my thoughts, my emotions, my reactions. That's why I was on another fucking retreat.

Why is it still so hard? I wondered. I had done 2,000 hours of training in holistic therapies, read countless books, gone on a dozen retreats, and spent four years in therapy and I was still struggling. Was I going to struggle forever? Would I ever feel better?

The days at the ranch were long and rigorous, with ten hours of meditation interrupted by meals and stretch breaks. Stillness was mandatory during meditation. I tried to convince my body to be calm, but it refused to cooperate. It burned constantly. I shook and cried on the cushion. I felt the same disassociation I'd felt in my father's house. I wasn't improving the way I hoped.

When I was leaving at the end of the week, Michael told me to come back again. He could help me get through it, he said. I should do the 90-day training.

What the hell, I thought, I don't have any other brilliant ideas. I agreed to return after my next trip to Scranton.

It was autumn and the leaves were turning orange, red, yellow, and brown during my next trip to Pennsylvania. I followed my father and Ann and the boys along a winding path in Serenity Forest, a "tranquil resting place" where tombstones were replaced with trees for an "uplifting memorial experience." The sky was blue with bright yellow sunlight.

"This is my tree." My father rested his hand on a tall maple with lush branches. "It's your place too, if you want." He' d found the forest on the internet. He seemed comforted by the idea of living in the body of a tree long after he was gone.

I stood a few feet away from the family, floating a bit in the ethers. The veil between the physical and non-physical felt thin and luminescent. My body tingled. I wondered if I'd be able to feel my father after he died the way I had felt my mother. The thought of it worried me.

On the way home, we stopped for an early dinner at his favorite Italian restaurant. We ate like ordinary people having an ordinary meal, but there was a sort of vacuum at the table. The life force was slowly draining out of the family.

Back at his house, we all retreated into our separate corners. I tried to practice the meditation I had learned from Michael. I sat with my eyes closed and felt a thousand unresolved hurts, everything I'd ever clung to.

I really wanted to forgive my father. As each stabbing pain surfaced, I imagined cutting the invisible cords which wove a sticky web around me.

I forgive you. I release you. I forgive you. I release you. I chanted until I was dizzy with exhaustion and finally fell asleep.

The next morning, I was frazzled from the nightmares that had haunted me during sleep. My reality seemed an indistinguishable mess of past and present, waking and dreaming. I felt more like a vapor than a solid human being.

Before my departure, I sat with Dad at the kitchen table again. He had the same pensive look. But this time, there was a different tone in his voice. "I'm leaving everything to Ann," he announced. "She'll manage all the assets and decide how things are distributed."

His words hit me like a sucker punch to the gut. For nearly forty years he had waved bank statements in my face, saying, "Look at all the millions I've made. I did this all for you. I'm putting the money away for you." Now he was trying to control my brother and me from the grave by leaving us in the hands of his most submissive wife.

"I'm sure you understand," he said.

My father cared nothing for my well-being, or anyone else's. My mother died with nothing but a dilapidated house, even though she was married to my father for a decade. His second wife was working at Walmart to make ends meet, even though she raised two of his children. It was sickening, but I was already so defeated I couldn't protest. My father had always been such a disappointment, that I discovered I wasn't even surprised.

When I returned home, I moved through my days like my boat in choppy water. Fever and seasickness were my companions. I forced myself to teach the online classes and give some massage therapy sessions. When the heat got so bad I couldn't eat or concentrate, I soothed my body with acupuncture or Reiki. I was waiting for the call from my brother, who was staying with Dad until the end. I kept checking the phone for messages or missed calls. My sleep was restless. My body flooded with adrenaline.

I woke one morning after a full moon night and noticed a text from my brother. Dad had passed.

I felt a strange flatness. There were no swirling energies. No hovering spirits. No transcendence of any kind. I felt no emotion, just the same unsteady rocking and waves of heat up and down my spine.

I hardly had any energy left to pretend to care about the funeral. The short guestlist assigned by Dad included a handful of family and friends. I followed everyone else on the same winding path in Serenity Forest. We arrived at the maple and found a dirt hole and a biodegradable urn with Dad's ashes. People said nice things about the devoted husband and father and doctor they were going to miss so much.

I wondered who they were talking about.

As soon as we got in the car, Joseph started unraveling about Dad's will. He had believed my father and the promise of inheritance, and he had already planned how he would spend the money. He was raging and grieving and falling apart. I felt a surge of sisterly love. I wanted to save him from the pain.

I returned with my brother to his apartment in the Bronx. I sat on the floor while he cried and punched the wall.

"Everything is going to be okay," I said. "We'll work it out."

He glared at me. "Why aren't you mad? Aren't you pissed?"

I shrugged. "Not really. Dad never did what he said he was gonna do. I guess I'm not surprised."

"But he promised us. I know he meant to leave it to us. He was just confused."

He wasn't confused. I thought. *He was a sociopath.*

I poured myself a glass of wine, climbed out onto the fire escape, and lit a cigarette. I could hear the neighbor's barking dog and Spanish music floating up from the bodega on the corner.

I thought about what I could do to make it better, to fill the gap left by my father and his betrayal and the lack of inheritance and the waves of pain plaguing us. Money had never meant much to me, but promises did. The promise of an inheritance, of the security and certainty and freedom we could have had as a result of the inheritance, meant something to me. The fact that my stepmother, who had known my father half-as-long as I had, was keeping all of his money, an estimated $50 million, for herself was an injustice.

Dad had always bribed us with money. He used it to manipulate his wives and children. Now, in his death, he was using money again to cause pain and suffering. Money was power. I was sick of being powerless, especially when it came to my father. I was sick of the idea that I needed a man for security, or that I couldn't protect the ones I loved because I didn't have enough money. I vowed that I would make it my mission, for the rest of my life if I had to, to make the money which had been promised to my brother and me. I would use that money to support myself and everyone I loved.

I'll figure out a way. I'll work harder. I'll work smarter.

I hadn't the faintest clue where to begin, but if my father could do it, so could I. Finance was as foreign to me as Chinese, but there was one thing I knew about myself: I never backed down from a challenge.

14

ON A WARM SUMMER night in 2014, the full moon shone bright over Manhattan. From my first visit to the Big Apple in middle school, the city never failed to inspire me. There was something about the skyscrapers, the lights on Broadway, and the Statue of Liberty that always made me feel like anything was possible. I was on my way to a networking event to find the next venture that would bring abundance to my life. I wore a bright yellow dress and strutted with confidence like I did on the same streets 20 years earlier as a fashion model.

I arrived at a towering building and rode the elevator up to a chic fitness studio with big windows and expensive equipment. Through sliding glass doors, I stepped onto a rooftop terrace overlooking Midtown. I walked around the perimeter of the pristine pool where vendors were giving away samples of luxury wellness products like organic nutrition bars and designer yoga clothes. Dozens of good-looking fitness people with bright white smiles mingled and chatted.

I was taste-testing different kinds of kombucha when a young guy standing next to me introduced himself as Jeremy. He looked more like a banker than a fitness trainer in his designer jeans and V-neck sweater. After we exchanged a little bit of small talk, I asked, "What do you do?"

"I'm the CEO of a start-up," he said.

That sounded promising. "What kind of startup?"

"It's a business networking site. I'm going to transform wellness at scale."

It sounded fancy, although I had no idea what it meant.

"What do you do?" he asked.

"I've been working in the wellness industry for twelve years as a massage therapist, yoga teacher, and university professor. I've had just about every job you can have in wellness from—"

"You should work for me!" Jeremy exclaimed. "I'm a business guy. I have an MBA. When I talk to wellness people, they look at me like I have three heads. I need a consultant who can give me insight into how wellness people think. I don't know what it's like to work as a yoga teacher or massage therapist, but you do!"

He was right. I knew more about health and wellness than just about anybody. We scheduled a day and time to meet.

Arriving at the open-plan workspace at Jeremy's company was like landing on a different planet. The loft was full of modern co-working desks, a messy kitchen, and dudes wearing jeans and sneakers. I spied Jeremy through a glass wall. He waved and smiled while talking on his phone and typing on his laptop. He motioned to a young blond girl to fetch me. After making espressos on an instant coffee machine, Kim took me into a conference space and set up the projector for Jeremy's presentation.

Jeremy talked fast and furiously about user experience, growth rates, ROI, digital customer acquisition, and so on. I could see why none of the wellness people had any idea what he was talking about.

After about twenty minutes of intense concentration, I finally figured out what his website was supposed to do to "transform wellness business." I got it. He wanted to make a one-stop-shop website.

"I can help you," I said, "but you should let me do the talking because it's really hard to understand what you're saying."

"Perfect! Let's do it."

Since my main residence was still my Miami boat, I rented a cheap room in the Chelsea neighborhood of New York City and went to the office every day. We had daily meetings in the conference room where Jeremy would rally the staff with grandiose exclamations.

"We're going to take over the world," Jeremy announced. "Who's ready to make millions?"

The team clapped.

"Are you ready? I don't think you're ready," he needled.

The team clapped louder and harder.

"We're not just a networking site. We're changing people's lives. We're changing the world. That's why you're here. That's what you're part of!"

Jeremy wanted to know what ideas we had that would *go viral* and *blow up the internet*.

My head was spinning when I left the meeting. Kim noticed my confusion. "All the start-up guys talk like that," she said. "You'll get used to it."

I was relieved that Kim was so down-to-earth and easy to talk to.

"I'm going to a women entrepreneur's event this weekend," she said. "You should come!"

"I'd love to!" I replied.

I arrived at a Midtown loft that weekend and smiling, happy girls greeted me at the door. Strings of lights and inspirational sayings hung on the wall behind them. The receptionist handed me a green tote bag filled with goodies. Kim waved to me from a beanbag chair. She was chatting with a girl with blue streaks in her hair and quirky round glasses.

Mary, the organizer, kicked off the day with a guided meditation and then announced a panel of "lady bosses." The panel consisted of beautiful women whose roles included computer programming, visual storytelling, digital marketing, and documentary filmmaking.

Before I left the event, I downloaded onto my phone a book that someone recommended, *Know Your Value: Women, Money, and Getting What You're Worth*, by Mika Brzezinski.

Let's do this, I thought. Show me the money!

When I got home from the conference, I curled up on the bed and read Mika's book cover-to-cover in a couple of hours. I went on Facebook to follow her page and noticed a post that read, "Win $10,000 in the Know Your Value Competition."

The only thing required to enter was a 1-minute video explaining why you deserved the money. I felt a flutter of butterflies in my belly. This felt meant to be. I wrote a short script, recorded it and uploaded it to the website. I was giddy when I hit the save button.

I continued to work at Jeremy's company. I was obsessed with learning as much as possible about tech, marketing, and business. Jeremy was in the process of raising more venture capital. He invited me to tag along to his investor meetings, where I learned just how stressful it is to be an entrepreneur. He confided in me that the jobs of all his employees were at stake. He needed the investment money so he could keep everyone employed. He felt responsible. He carried the weight of that with him. I'd never thought of it that way. I was glad it wasn't me in the hot seat.

One morning at work, I received a cryptic email from an MSNBC producer. They asked me to call a number because they had some questions. A woman named Janet picked up the phone on the first ring and said, "We need you to answer some questions. Can we Skype with you tomorrow?"

Excited but confused, I said, "Sure." My heart was doing flips in my chest. It would be a miracle to win $10,000 and to be on national TV!

I couldn't sleep that night. I kept thinking about the email, the call, the conversation with Janet. I played it over and over in my mind. I pictured myself onstage on TV, accepting the prize.

At nine the next morning, I was sitting at my laptop, visibly trembling and sweating, when the call came in. A charming reporter appeared on the screen. The backdrop was the MSNBC news desk.

"Hey, Dr. Gabby, so nice to meet you!" she said. "I have someone who wants to talk to you."

Dr. Gabby. I liked the sound of that.

As she slid out of the seat and Mika took her place, I felt a wave of exhilaration.

"Dr. Gabby," she said.

"Hey, Mika!" I was practically yelling.

"You're a finalist in the Know Your Value Competition. Can you join me in Washington DC next month?"

"Yes, of course! Thank you so much!"

After the call ended, I jumped up and down. It felt like everything was falling into place.

A week later, I gasped as I walked into the lobby of Washington D.C.'s Marriott Marquis. The walls were fifteen stories of glass. At the center within them was a massive sculpture that looked like a dancing angel. I followed the signs to the main ballroom, where a busy crew was setting up hundreds of chairs, a long platform stage, TV cameras, and big blinding lights.

A rush of production staff, photographers, and other people swirled around me. I felt like a celebrity. A flurry of instructions came at me from all directions—where to go, what to say, when to start. There were two other candidates competing for the same $10,000 prize. We three women would have costume changes and on-camera interviews. At the end of the day, we would give our sixty-second pitch on stage to Mika and the judges. There would only be one winner.

The ballroom was filled with hundreds of women who shared my mission of owning their value and making more money. Brooke Shields and Elizabeth Warren offered inspiring speeches. My eyes filled with tears. I couldn't believe it was actually happening after the horrible year I'd had.

After a frenzy of activity on and off camera, the moment finally came for the contestants to take our places on the stage in the ballroom. Mika rallied the crowd.

"Are we ready to hear the pitches? Are we going to be supportive? Are you feeling it for them?" she asked.

The audience roared with cheers and applause.

I took the long, steady walk up the aisle with my two competitors, Kara and Kay. Kara was a breast cancer survivor who made customized bras for mastectomy patients. Kay was a military vet who taught hip-hop dance to inner-city kids.

The air was electric. I felt like I was floating. As I felt the love radiating from the audience, I felt completely in tune with the world around me, like I was exactly where I was supposed to be.

I stepped into the spotlight, lifted the mic to my mouth, and said, "We all face formidable challenges in our lives, some bigger than others, like suicidal depression or discrimination. I've made it my life's work to help people overcome those challenges. I want this bonus so that I can build an online school that offers classes at affordable prices to anyone with internet access. This competition has made me realize that my true value comes from giving people tools to transform their lives. And with your support, we can grow that value together." I was confident. I was poised. I knew exactly what I wanted to say, and I nailed it.

After I stepped back to my place, Kara gave her pitch and then Kay. They both did a great job, too.

The judges deliberated for some time. Then Mika announced the winner. "And the winner of the $10,000 bonus is...Kay Brown!"

I was so bummed. I really thought I was going to win.

As I climbed down off the stage and into the crowd, women from the audience gathered around me.

"We liked you best!" they said. "You should've won!"

I savored their validation and admiration.

One woman approached me and handed me her business card. "Call me," she said. "I want to invest in your idea."

Her offer eased my disappointment at not winning the prize.

I followed my new friends into the lobby bar. We each grabbed a glass of champagne and stood around in a circle. Glasses clinked as we toasted to our happiness and success.

"Congratulations!" someone shouted.

"To knowing our value!" we cheered.

For the next year, I split my time between New York and Miami. I was on a mission to build a successful business and achieve financial freedom. Like a diver searching for treasure, I swam into the depths of the internet. I clicked on every link, scrolled every website, dove into multiple e-courses and entrepreneurial books, capturing anything I could get my hands on that might lead me closer to quick and easy prosperity.

I fired off emails to all my former students, announcing my plans for an online school. Almost immediately, I heard back from Lily.

She said, "You know my history of growing up as an obese kid and how it has affected my life. I got this idea that I wanted to work as a health coach. I have one client, and I've really enjoyed working with her. I've got a lot of ideas about other things I'd like to do, but I can't seem to get it together. I have this unrelenting fear that I'm too old and people won't take me seriously. I'm scared to put myself out there. I'm pissed off at myself, and I constantly feel like I'm running out of time."

I called Lily. We had a long talk about the kinds of tools and support that she needed to move forward. I could hear the pain in her voice and I desperately wanted to help her.

I created an online course called *Women in Wellness Career Training,* with a 100-page companion e-book called *Blissful Business: A Gorgeous Guide to Creating Your Dream Career in Health & Wellness.*

I imagined thousands of women flocking to join and hundreds of thousands of dollars flowing into my bank account.

Eight former students agreed to beta-test the course. Each week, I guided them through all the aspects of creating a wellness career. The feedback was overwhelmingly positive. I felt like I was finally using everything I'd learned from my education and experience to create the ideal offering.

Lily's despair turned into enthusiasm. She sent me a message saying, "I love the course, and I look forward to the conference calls with you every week. I no longer feel lost. You answered all my questions and gave me valuable information that I can apply immediately to move forward. Thank you very much for being an inspiration."

Lily's gratitude was what I needed to keep the momentum going. I reached out to various organizations and started giving talks. I got bookings in Miami, New York, Los Angeles, and even a Caribbean Cruise. I shared about my journey from modeling to earning my Ph.D., to building an online business and my experience at the Know Your Value competition. I was interviewed on the radio and on podcasts.

With each event and media appearance, more and more women joined my community. My business was growing right before my eyes. All those long hours on the laptop were paying off—but not enough. I was spending more money on travel and operations than I was making. I wasn't any closer to my goal than when I started.

One morning, I was talking with Lily on the phone about her coaching business. She'd had a great week. Lots of people had called her in crisis, and she was able to give them life-saving advice. She explained how validating it was to know that she could provide so much value.

I asked her how much money she had made.

"None," she said.

"None?" I asked.

She told me how much her clients really needed her, how they couldn't afford to pay, and that she couldn't leave them bleeding on the side of the road.

"Lily, you've invested so much time and money into your education. You told me that you wanted to expand your practice, and this is the perfect opportunity. Empathy makes you a great coach, but it also makes you vulnerable to giving away the goods for free," I counseled.

"I'm still trying to figure out what to do," she hedged.

"It doesn't have to be complicated," I urged her. "Just start charging what you're worth."

I felt a subtle irritation stirring inside. I had been mentoring Lily for months, and she always had an excuse about charging for her services. She was plagued with self-doubt and inhibition. And I didn't know how to help her if she wouldn't take my advice.

Unlike Lily, I was chasing clients and money relentlessly. I promoted my business nonstop online and offline—often foregoing meals and sleep and working around-the-clock. I felt a visceral sense of urgency, like I needed to reach my goals as soon as possible.

In my other consulting calls, I heard the same procrastination and inhibition from my clients. They promised they would act, but they never did. Month after month, they would have fabulous reasons why it wasn't the right time - it was the holidays, it was the credit card debt, it was the lack of credentials—and their dreams would be postponed again.

My irritation grew stronger. Indecision. Perfectionism. Procrastination. Anxiety. These obstacles surfaced for my clients repeatedly, and I didn't know what to do to help overcome them.

One day, I was stressing over my predicament when an unexpected email from a book publisher arrived in my inbox. It said they were "interested in discussing potential projects."

OMG! This is the break I've been waiting for! I jumped up and down after I read the message.

I added the writing project to my already full plate. I spent the next few months flying to conferences, giving talks, and making contacts while maintaining full operations and writing from midnight until two in the morning. I posted all my adventures on social media, trying to compete with the other glamourous entrepreneurs.

The more that my image looked "fabulous and free," the more confined I felt by responsibility and obligations. I made it look easy. I made it look fun. But it was not as easy or fun as it looked. I was glued to my computer and phone at all times. I was up at four in the morning on the west coast to prepare for 7 a.m. calls on the East Coast. I paid for all my travel out of pocket. My minimal savings was dwindling fast, increasing my panic and churning stomach. I worked tirelessly to maintain my perfect reputation. I wouldn't dare do anything to tarnish that image.

It doesn't have to feel good, I told myself. It just has to work.

At one of the conferences in California, I met Sarah, a literary agent for a prestigious agency in NYC. She was excited to represent me and my book project. I couldn't believe my luck. Not only did she facilitate the meeting with the publisher who contacted me, but she set up several calls with other major publishers. I wondered how much money they would pay me and how many books we'd sell. I couldn't wait to see my book on the *New York Times* bestseller list. I was spinning with desire and fantasy and the promise of bounty.

After each one of the calls, I waited with bated breath for an offer. One by one, we heard back from the publishers. "Dr. Gabby is amazing, but she doesn't have enough social media followers."

"We LOVE Dr. Gabby. Call us back when she has 100,000 people on her mailing list."

"We love your work, your energy, and your writing. We know that your book will find a good home."

Even the publisher who had initially reached out changed their mind when they reviewed the book proposal. With each rejection, I felt more defeated and despondent. I had no idea how I could continue to do everything I was already doing *and* get one hundred thousand followers. If the publishers loved me and my book, why wouldn't they publish it? I needed to start making more money right away. I wondered how I was going to do that without a book to reach people beyond my own small circle of current clients.

When I got back to Miami, I had to haul the boat out of the water to replace broken parts and take the car in for an expensive repair. It would have been manageable if I hadn't spent thousands of dollars on travel and book preparations, but my dreams were costing me much more than I'd anticipated. At nighttime, my panic returned as my mind spun all kinds of horrible future scenarios of being destitute and alone.

I felt my wounds surfacing and my self-esteem plummeting. Messages from clients asking for help filled my inbox. Like water filling up the boat, each email I removed was replaced with another. I thought about money constantly. I started listening to metaphysical recordings about the Law of Attraction and thought that maybe I could manifest the money I needed.

On the outside, I looked like a wildly successful woman, Hundreds of women eagerly listened to and appreciated my advice. I couldn't tell anyone the truth about how badly I was struggling, which only made it harder to keep going. I would be an outcast if anyone actually knew I was a fraud.

While I was in New York for an event, I received several messages from my clients. Jessica got her first article published. Kenia was invited to speak at a national corporate event. Veronica finally launched her online course. They were so happy and grateful. They credited me with the inspiration and guidance they needed to accomplish their goals.

I wanted to feel proud of myself. I wanted to feel fulfilled. But I read each email with bittersweet emotion. The pursuit of money was a pain, not a pleasure. I was hanging on by my fingernails to keep going with the façade of ease and success while hiding the truth of my panic and fatigue. Lifting these women up—lifting everyone up for my whole life—was not uplifting me.

I was empty. I never said no. I was always taking care of everyone else instead of taking care of myself. I wasn't sure I even knew how to take care of myself. I didn't even want to try and make money anymore. I just wanted it to appear.

I imagined a wealthy man sweeping off my feet, taking me on fabulous trips, and having an epic romance. It had been a few years since I broke up with Karl. I was ready for another romance.

The following day when I checked my email, there was a message from Rick, the owner of the rehab whom I'd briefly dated in Los Angeles a decade earlier. I remembered the hikes we took in the redwood forest, and the laughter we shared before I had to drive cross-country to start my teaching job at Georgian Court University. The thought of him made me smile. We had lost touch long ago, but I was curious about what he had been doing all this time. If I wasn't mistaken, I thought I saw wedding photos of him on social media. Surely, he wasn't reaching out for a date.

His message said that he had purchased a luxury retreat property in Northern California and he needed a Program Director.

"With your experience and education, I thought you might be interested. If so, please email or call, and if not, I wish you all the best," he said.

Rick's email stopped me cold. It sounded like everything I'd been waiting for. *Was this the miracle I'd been trying to manifest?*

Just like that, I was willing to abandon two years of entrepreneurship to run into the arms of fate.

Only I never stopped to ask, Is this fate a blessing or a curse?

15

WHEN I ARRIVED AT the majestic property in the redwood forest about 20 minutes north of Silicon Valley in July of 2017 it was so surreal, I thought I was dreaming. The grounds were spectacular: twenty-four luxury treehouses surrounded by a three-story main house with winding paths, a walking labyrinth, an indoor pool, and hot tub. I could hardly believe it. It wasn't just the beauty of the place that astounded me. A concentration of energy, like a spiritual vortex, permeated everything and made me feel like I was floating out of my body.

I was greeted in the lobby by Tony and Alice, an older married couple who were living on the property. They showed me to my room, a corner unit with a king-size bed, big bright windows, and a bathtub the size of my boat. It was cozy and serene, decorated with soft colors and natural wood.

I wondered what it would be like to see Rick again. Was he still cute? Would I even recognize him? In our brief call, he'd told me that in the nine years since we'd last seen each other he had gotten married, had a son, and gotten divorced. His ex-wife and child were living in

Casper, Wyoming, and he was commuting back-and-forth to Woodside for work. I hoped he'd called not only because he wanted my help with his business, but also to rekindle what we'd started long ago.

Rick walked into the room with lines around his eyes and a beard hugging his face. He looked like an animal in need of rescue, worn and tattered, tattooed with shame and loneliness. A wave of compassion mixed with lust and trepidation washed over me. We shook hands and had an awkward conversation along the lines of, nice to see you; thanks for coming.

I was relieved when he suggested that we go out to dinner to catch up. We sat in a sushi restaurant for a couple of hours, and he recounted his wife's infidelity and the demise of his marriage.

I felt sorry for him. "It's not your fault," I said.

Something about him reminded me of my father, but I couldn't put my finger on it. His gestures, maybe. The tone of his voice. Instead of being scared, I was intrigued. I leaned in closer. Our conversation lasted late into the night.

The next day we went for a hike around the property. The smell of the redwood forest was as intoxicating as when I had visited the first time, more than fifteen years earlier, for the CIIS retreats. I felt at home among the trees—happy and energized, eager to start a new adventure with Rick. Our day was filled with laughter, and I was relieved to see him smile.

Maybe I can fix him, I thought. Maybe I can heal him and build a wildly successful business at the same time.

I should've seen the signs of codependency and my obsession to be worthy, but I didn't. I slipped into a trance, convinced that this was my dream come true. My ache for salvation was still stronger than my awareness of the consequences of my choices.

On our second night together, we made dinner in the kitchen. It was effortless and fun. I felt the chemistry and connection growing between me and Rick. I had already accepted the position as Program Director. I would leave in the morning, go back to Miami for my things, and then drive back to California. I felt like the whole transition couldn't happen fast enough. I didn't even want to leave.

"I wanna show you something." I pulled out a CD and put it in the stereo. "Do you remember this?" I asked.

We sat in the dark, listening to the songs.

Rick said, "You kept this? I can't believe you kept this."

It was a CD he had made for me after our dates in Los Angeles.

"Of course, I kept it. It's a great CD."

He smiled. "Wanna go in the hot tub?"

As we floated in the steaming water drinking red wine, I was hot and dizzy and bursting with impatience. We talked about every possible thing until there was nothing left to talk about.

I was so distracted by his lips that I could barely focus on the words coming out of his mouth. I desperately wanted to kiss him. We would both be leaving the property in a few hours. I couldn't bear to separate without touching him. I threw my arms around his neck. We were transported back in time to when our whole world was easy and fun and full of possibilities. I felt like I'd waited a long time for him—maybe my whole life.

"I wasn't ready for you then," Rick said. "But I'm ready now." There was a sincerity in his eyes that made it easy to believe him.

We tumbled into bed, ravenous and desperate for each other. I fell asleep in his arms. He stroked my hair and kissed me on the head when he left in the morning.

I was in love. Rick was the one.

The drop into backwoods life was disorienting. I moved from a boat into a treehouse. Instead of abundant marine life, my company was spiders, banana slugs, and the occasional snake or mountain lion. Rick was mostly in Wyoming, and I ached for him. Each time he visited, I felt intoxicated with love and affection. When he left, a deep emptiness followed. The bipolarity of our affair was familiar. It reminded me of Dad, how he had a family I wasn't part of, how I wanted more than anything to fill the void of family and belonging.

In the days while Rick was away, I binged on work. I had the monumental task of building a business from scratch again like I had in Miami a few years earlier. Only this time, I needed a chef and hiking guides and massage therapists, and so much more. It was both exhilarating and daunting. I gathered all parts of myself, from the academic to the healer to the entrepreneur, stretching and expanding myself to the limits. Creative energies flowed through me as never before.

My energy plus Rick's energy plus the energy of the property swirled in an explosion of ideas, inspiration, and action. I was wholly driven by love, purpose, and passion. I woke in the middle of the night with visions of lectures, activities, and exercises to transform guests' lives. I felt like everything I had done for my entire life had been leading up to this moment.

Rick didn't always share my enthusiasm for my ideas. When I told him what supplies we needed, his face grew red, and his hands were sweaty. He rubbed his forehead like I was giving him a headache. I didn't understand why he was so upset and wondered if I was doing something wrong. I only wanted to please him and make him happy. I apologized even when I didn't know what I was apologizing for.

Rick had type 1 diabetes. I knew that his mood might fluctuate with his blood sugar, so I offered massages and nutritious meals to help him feel better. I did everything I could to ensure a healthy and harmonious dynamic.

Rick sent two of his friends from Wyoming to help me set up the center. After a long day of work, we lit a fire and poured some whiskey.

One of the guys started ranting about Rick's ex. "She's sleeping with every guy in Casper."

His words cut through me.

Maybe that was why Rick was so worried. Maybe things were really bad in Wyoming. I could love him better than she did. I could prove to him that love didn't have to be painful or hard. I'd show him that happiness was possible.

When Rick visited the following week, I gently brought it up. "Jason said some things about Karen. Is everything okay in Casper?"

Rick's jaw tightened. "Everything is fine," he said. "I don't want you to worry about that stuff."

After some gentle nudging, he told me about a rock-bottom night of whisky and crying after he caught Karen cheating. He considered suicide but realized that he had to stay alive to take care of his son.

Rick said, "Did I tell you about the birth? It was really difficult. The cord was wrapped around his neck. Karen had a really hard time. She was hooked up to all kinds of machines. I went with Simon to the ICU. His little hand held my finger. I sang 'Hey Jude' to him to comfort him. He loves the song now. He sings it with me."

The story moved through me like an immense wave. I focused on my breath and counted backward from ten. I would cry about it later, but I wanted to smile for Rick so he would keep opening up to me. I wanted to be everything that he wanted and needed.

"Are you okay with me telling you this stuff?" he asked.

"Of course," I lied. It made me so uncomfortable to hear the intimate details of his wife and child when we were so fresh in love.

"I know that it's heavy," he said.

"Maybe it sucked for you guys," I joked, "but it worked out great for me because now I get to be with you."

He laughed a big belly laugh and squeezed my hand as if to say thank you.

On the first day of the first retreat, Rick's family and friends gathered at the center to experience the program I'd created. In a matter of weeks, I had put together a staff and curriculum and bought everything we needed for the guests. The program was built on four pillars—food, movement, rest, and happiness. Each day was filled with hikes, massages, and scrumptious farm-to-table meals.

That evening we gathered in the dining room for live music and mocktails. I was trembling with joy and anxiety as Rick introduced me to his parents. Would they like and accept me? Could they be my new family? I hoped so.

I had notecards and pens set on a table and invited everyone to write their intentions for the weekend—what they wanted to receive, what they wanted to give. I hung the notecards on the branches of a centerpiece arrangement. Colorful words dangled like prayer flags among us. *Peace. Healing. Positive energy.*

We moved into the garden for dinner. A long, decorated table lit by candles and outdoor string lights set the mood for intimate conversation and connection. As I looked around at the smiling faces, I filled with happiness and pride.

How did I get so lucky?

The following day, my staff and I guided the guests through yoga, cooking demos, rigorous fitness, and rejuvenating spa treatments. As each hour passed, the intensity increased. We had to meet their every need perfectly, from the room temperature to food allergies to minor injuries to lost objects. The property was massive, and I ran from one side to the other from sunrise until sunset. We were on a tight schedule and had to maintain high energy at all times. There was no time for resting, and no room for mistakes.

Hungry for Rick's validation and approval, I watched his eyes for clues about his impression. His ease and laughter were encouraging. I prayed that the experience was exactly what he wanted it to be.

On the final day, we gathered as a group and discussed what we had learned and how we had changed as a result of the retreat. The faces were brighter. The smiles were bigger. Rick's family and friends said that it was a powerful, uplifting experience, and that it exceeded their expectations. Their gratitude and appreciation brought tears to my eyes. I felt like I had been holding my breath for days, waiting for the results of a life-or-death test, and I could finally exhale.

After the guests left and I got into bed with Rick, I wept with relief. "What's wrong?" he asked.

"It was just so much pressure. It was just...so much."

"You never have to worry." He hugged me tightly. "You're safe with me. You did an incredible job. You're the most amazing woman I've ever met."

It was everything I ever wanted to hear, a promise I never got from my father, or any other man in my life.

Before Rick left to return to Wyoming, he told me a realtor would be showing the property to a prospective buyer. He assured me that it was just a formality, part of a settlement agreement that he had with the local community. I didn't understand the explanation, but I didn't question it. I knew we had created something magical—both professionally and personally - that would last for years to come.

Immediately, I got busy preparing for the next set of guests. I had invited friends from New York, Miami, and Los Angeles to participate. I had only been at the retreat center for 3 months and we already had a world-class program. I was so proud and I wanted everyone to bear witness.

The day before we were to begin, raging wildfires swept across Northern California. The air was filled with smoke, and thousands of people were evacuated.

Rick called. He was opening the center to forty displaced addicts who needed a place to stay. This new responsibility felt overwhelming as I wondered how I was going to run a wellness retreat and take care of the addiction group.

We brought in extra staff and set up a second dining room in a meeting space on the first floor. We rearranged accommodations and made alternative plans for activities.

I felt even more worried than before about making a good impression and proving to Rick that I could perform under pressure. We had some stressful conversations about the situation, and I forced myself to be cheerful and accommodating. I fumbled through the weekend, feeling extreme highs and lows. I was still consumed with the need for things to be flawless. My friends who were doing the program glowed with excitement and appreciation. They had no idea the burden that I was carrying.

Rick noticed my tension and inquired about it.

"I'm fine," I said.

"No, you're not. Tell me what's wrong."

I willed myself to keep all my emotions tightly contained, but they spilled out like an open bag of marbles. "It's just that...you're here, and then you're going to leave...and I'm here all the time without you. And I miss you so much. I want to do a good job. I want you to be happy... How come you never invite me to Wyoming? Am I ever going to see where you live, or meet your son?"

Rick froze in his chair.

"You want to come to Wyoming?" he asked.

"Yeah, of course."

"I didn't know you wanted to come."

It was so hard to tell Rick what I wanted. I didn't want to pressure him, or nag. I knew he was pulled in many different directions—he told me as much when the business tasks were piling up. I didn't want to be one more thing on his to-do list.

"Okay, I'll get you a ticket for next week," he said.

I couldn't tell from the emotion in my body if I had won or lost. Why did I feel so uncomfortable if I had gotten what I wanted? Was Rick just placating me? Did he really want me to come? I decided to ignore my feelings and make my travel plans.

When I arrived in the cowboy airport of Casper, Wyoming, the roads were covered in a blanket of snow. Rick exuded the confidence of a mountain man in his beat-up Bronco and his flannel shirt—he was at ease and had nothing to prove. He hugged me tightly and said, "Thanks for coming."

The single dad was a side of Rick I had never seen before. I tried to reconcile it with the LA playboy, and the real estate developer.

Walking into his house was like worlds colliding. I knew his ex-used to live there with him. It was where he'd caught her cheating. I had shoes to fill, a past to overcome, and a future to build. It made me unsteady on my feet.

Rick was a gracious host. He gave me a tour of the small town and took me to the local hot springs. We floated in the sulfur waters, ate a long, lingering meal at the best restaurant in town, drank wine, and talked for hours. The intimacy between us was fast and fierce. My previous life and aspirations faded into the background as I became more attached to Rick and moved completely into his world.

I expected to meet Simon, but Rick wasn't ready. After two nights, I returned to California feeling like we had made some progress, but we still had a long way to go. Rick was spoiling me and keeping me at a distance simultaneously. I told myself to hang on. My habit of impatience would only disrupt the harmony between us.

We closed the center for the holidays, planning an official launch for January. Every few days, the realtor passed through with a prospective buyer. A tech mogul who wanted an incubator. A nonprofit that needed an ashram. A wealthy couple that wanted a private residence. Tony and Alice would scurry around the property, turning on lights and dusting off furniture when they came through.

I asked Rick if he would ever consider selling the center.

"It would have to be a big offer, at least thirty million dollars," he said. "Everything is for sale at the right price."

His nonchalance made me tremble. I had moved my whole life to this place. I would be homeless and jobless if he sold it. How could he even consider selling it when we had barely gotten the business off the ground? My face crumpled into a frown.

"Don't worry," Rick assured me. "It's only a probability, not even a possibility. You'll be the first to know if anything changes."

Rick whisked me off on a luxury vacation to Mexico. He planned the whole affair, from swimming with sharks to nightclub reservations in Cabo. He ordered couples massages and bought me gifts in the shops. The extravagance overwhelmed me.

"I want to know everything about you," he said.

I told him about my adventures in the years that we were apart. He looked at me with reverent disbelief, like I was some sort of fallen angel who'd landed in his lap.

"I'm a lucky man," he said.

I thought I was the lucky one, the luckiest girl in the world. I wanted the relationship to work. I needed to be with Rick forever.

One evening on the trip, Rick did a Facetime call with his son. He snuck off to do these meetings sometimes when we were at the center, but this was the first time I was close to the conversation. He sat on the balcony in his swimsuit, purring into the phone, gushing with loving comments, saying, "Daddy misses you so much. I can't wait to see you."

After he hung up, a flurry of hateful messages lit up his phone. Karen was angry. How could he be so disrespectful? How could he be naked on the call? How could he be with his disgusting girlfriend on vacation in Mexico, the place they used to visit together.

Rick was mystified by her rant. It had been a year since the divorce. Why did she care?

Rick told me that Karen had been following me on social media. She was jealous and resentful. He felt bad for her and hoped she would move on. This felt far too familiar as I flashed back to Mom and Dad and being handed off for visitation. I recalled the time Dad showed up with my pregnant stepmom. Mom had called her a whore, and Dad had told my mother she was crazy.

I felt the same tension and decomposing love between Rick and Karen that I felt between my parents. If these were red flags about my future with Rick, I willfully ignored them and focused on the pleasure of our blissful vacation.

Rick asked me to spend Christmas with his family at their cabin in Nevada. My heart thumped as I eagerly agreed. I felt as if he was asking me to marry him. It had been years since I'd spent Christmas with a family. Most of my holidays were spent alone or at parties with friends. For the first time in a long time, I thought I might have found my happily ever after.

Rick and I picked up his son at his ex's house in Casper before making the short flight to Vegas. I sat nervously in the car while Rick went to the door. Karen and her boyfriend came out, and we exchanged artificial smiles and greetings. Rick put Simon in the car seat and attempted to drive away, but we were lodged in a snowbank. Rick told me to get in the driver's seat while he got out to push. I pressed on the gas while the other three adults rocked the Bronco back and forth. Simon cried in the car seat behind me.

Suddenly, the tires caught some traction. Snow spewed all over Karen's face, and the car lunged forward.

Rick was laughing when he got back in the car. "Did you see that?" he asked. "She was covered in snow. That was hilarious."

I was so relieved to be going to Nevada, far away from Karen and Casper. I didn't want to be part of the drama between miserable ex-lovers. I wanted the merriest Christmas ever.

The cabin was a cozy, rustic house in a quiet neighborhood. A lush Christmas tree posed in the living room corner, with piles of presents beneath it. I felt right at home with Rick's mom and sister as we prepped dinner and made small talk in the kitchen. Rick was preoccupied with Simon, hovering over the toddler's every move like a helicopter.

I was shocked at how difficult it was to get any attention from Rick while we were with his son. I wanted to connect with both of them, to feel the warmth of our threesome. I tried to insert myself as much as possible, offering gifts and toys to Simon, but I felt myself falling short. I spent a lot of time looking at the back of Rick's head while he was engaged with Simon. It gave me an empty, lonely sort of feeling.

I was reassured when Rick gave me a Christmas card that said, *I want you to know how much I love you and how much you mean to me. The happiness you create by just being in my space. The warmth and affection when you touch me. The calmness and awareness I have when you see me getting worked up. No one else has ever made me feel that way or has ever made me feel the connection I have with you. I know that I am not easy, and I know that I make things more difficult with my stubbornness. I want to try to be better because you deserve the best that I can be. I hope that we have many, many, many happy times, and that we will be together for as long as you will put up with me.*

His words were like sunshine on a dark day. The distance between us closed. My world was spinning right and smooth again.

After all the presents were opened and the ball had dropped from the flagpole in Times Square, Rick and I returned to the center in California. I was eager to get back to business. I had so many ideas about how we could market and sell the program. I was ready to fill up every room and retreat with new guests. Rick stalled however, dragging his feet for some unknown reason.

"I'm not sure we should keep working together," he said.

I felt the rumble of an avalanche move through me.

"Now that we're involved, I don't know if it's a good idea." Rick's eyes roamed the room, looking everywhere but at me.

I frowned. "I don't understand."

"My attorney says it's a liability. That I'm putting myself at risk."

I frowned. "What risk? What do you think I'm going to do?"

"There could be a lawsuit," he said.

"You think I'm going to sue you? For what?" I couldn't imagine a world in which I would cause Rick harm.

He gave cryptic answers. Perspiration beaded on his brow.

It was getting late, and we put the conversation to bed. My chest was tight and my emotions erratic. It was difficult to sleep. Is he ever going to trust me? What do I have to do to prove my loyalty to him? I wondered.

It never occurred to me to consider what he had to do to prove his loyalty to me.

16

BAD DECISIONS ALWAYS LOOK obvious in retrospect. Staring in the rear-view mirror of my life, Rick is one of my biggest regrets. But even if I could go back and get the attention of the stubborn woman I was and tell her what was about to happen, she wouldn't have believed me.

Instead of admitting the glaring red flags and fleeing Rick's property after our conversation, I pretended that it never happened. The following day, Rick gave me the green light to move forward and I threw myself into work, hustling in every way I knew how to grow the business as if it were my own child. I knew in my soul that I could make the business successful. I drove up and down the avenues of Silicon Valley, introducing myself to the VC and tech firms. I made phone calls, sent emails, invited journalists and travel agents to the property. I was bingeing on Law of Attraction lectures and intoxicated with the vortex of the property.

When I brought the first corporate booking proposal to Rick, he lashed out at me and told me that it wasn't what he wanted. "I'm the boss!" he shouted.

I retreated to my room, shaking and confused. How could he yell at me like that? Why was he being so mean? I focused on my breath and meditated myself into a place of serenity as I prayed for calmness and peace.

A few hours later, Rick came into the room like a dog with his tail between his legs.

"I don't want to be disrespectful," he said.

"I understand."

"I'm tired." He rubbed his beard with a sigh.

"What do you need?"

Instead of giving him the cold shoulder like his ex would have done, I gave him a massage and reassured him that I wasn't upset. My mission was to vibrate as much love and kindness as possible.

Rick permitted me to book the retreat. It was thousands of dollars— the biggest sale of my life. After that, I was unstoppable. I sold more and more group retreats. Twelve-thousand. Thirty-thousand. Sixty-thousand dollars! Rick was astonished. Each sale was a monumental victory for me—proof of my value, the security of the center, the glue that would keep Rick and me together.

"No one has ever made this property profitable," he said. "You are unbelievable."

I was thrilled. As long as I could keep the money flowing in, everything would be ok.

To celebrate our success and our one-year anniversary, Rick whisked me off on another trip. He booked us a suite at the Bellagio in Vegas and took me race car driving at the track. I sped around the course in an orange McLaren, dizzy with speed and satisfaction. We indulged in top-rated French cuisine and a show on the strip. Rick gave me a dozen roses and a handwritten card that said, *You are the love of my life. Thank you so much for being amazing, patient, strong, vulnerable, intelligent, beautiful, supportive, understanding, challenging, flexible, sexy...basically, everything I want and need.*

I snuggled with him in bed, revealing deeper bits of my personal history. The more I shared, the more he held me like he never wanted to let me go. I was high on our love. I thanked the gods for bringing him into my life.

After a few more weeks of regular operations at the center, Rick started stalling me again. I sent him a few proposals, and he was reluctant to sign off. I worried that his reservations about our professional relationship were returning.

One afternoon, Rick said, "We need to talk."

Every muscle in my body tightened. I held my breath.

"Remember when I told you that you would be the first to know if we had a buyer for the property?"

The room started to spin. My legs felt weak. Quiet seconds ticked by. "You sold the center," I said.

"I have a letter of intent from a buyer. The deal isn't done yet, but if everything goes well, it should be finished in three months."

I felt like I was going to vomit. Next to the death of my parents, this was the worst news of my life. The programs I created at the retreat center were my biggest accomplishment, the best of everything I had to offer. I thought I was going to be there for decades, sharing it with as many people as possible.

"When did this happen?" I asked.

"We've been going back and forth since January," he said.

I wanted to scream, *Eight months?! All this time I was working so hard and you were stalling. And I thought I was doing something wrong...While I thought we were building a forever business, you were talking to them behind my back. That's why you thought I would sue you. I'll be jobless and homeless in three months! What the hell am I going to do?*

187

"What about us? What are we going to do?" I asked calmly.

"I'm going to go back to Wyoming to raise my son."

"And what about me?" I asked.

He stared at the floor. I heard the words he wasn't saying.

"You want me to move to Wyoming."

"I don't want you to do anything you don't want to do." His eyes were still pinned to the ground.

Rick embraced me. Kissed me. I tried to play it cool. But how could I live in Wyoming, with him and Karen and all the drama and pain? What about my career? How could he do this to me? My body exploded in painful protest. I was nauseous. Adrenaline flooded me. I could feel a burning sensation everywhere. A life without the retreat center and Rick seemed unimaginable.

Everything was breaking inside me as Rick undressed me and got on top of me. I flooded his kisses with tears as I heaved with inconsolable grief. He let me cry for a few minutes, waiting for the storm to pass.

When it must have seemed like it was taking longer than necessary, he said, "This is hard for me, too. Don't make me feel guilty."

His words shut me down. I went numb from head to toe. I remembered how my mom fell apart after Dad divorced her, how she sat with legs intertwined at the kitchen table smoking cigarettes, and slept for days at a time. How she never found another partner after the loss of the love of her life. How she died a decade later, alone. I felt the raw bleeding place inside of me widen and expand.

That will be me. I'll never get over Rick.

I swallowed the sobs. I'm going to surrender, I thought. I'm going to let him have his way. He is my family now. Sometimes you have to make sacrifices for what you love. I love him and I need him, and I'm never going to leave him.

"Okay," I said. "What do you need me to do?"

Over the next few days, Rick transformed into a madman on a mission to strip the property of assets and close the deal with the buyer. The negotiations needed to remain top secret until papers were signed and checks were cashed. I wasn't allowed to make any more bookings or talk to staff about what was happening.

I became an imposter in my own life, denying my own needs as I devoted myself entirely to Rick's agenda. I clenched every muscle to hold in my anguish. I walked around the center in a daze, unable to look my employees in the eye for fear that they would see my duplicity.

Sometimes, I drove the backroads of Northern California and screamed at the top of my lungs, loud and ugly, just to release some of the pressure. It felt like there wasn't enough space in my body to hold the explosion that was detonating.

I longed to feel close to Rick, to maintain our intense intimacy and affection. But there were no more nights of long, lingering dinners or sensual soaks in the hot tub. Our romance was completely eclipsed by mandatory inventory documents and packing boxes of equipment.

One evening, when he was plundering the property like a hurricane, I asked him to stop, to pay some attention to me. "Can we go out?" I asked. "We don't do anything fun anymore."

His eyes filled red with rage, and his voice turned icy cold. "This isn't working. We made a good effort. We gave it a good shot. But it's over now," he said.

I felt 1,000 knives stabbing my gut.

"What are you talking about?"

"I'm done."

"Done with what?" I asked. After a pause, I asked, "Are you breaking up with me?"

"Yes."

I felt like I was freezing and burning simultaneously. The pain was unbearable. "This is ridiculous," I said. "We are not breaking up. We're never breaking up."

"Yes, we are."

I stayed calm. I held my breath. If I don't freak out, maybe he'll take it back, I thought.

Rick went to take a shower as if we'd had the most ordinary conversation in the world. I sat dumbfounded on the bed for fifteen minutes, my body burning, my mind spinning. I shoved my panic as far down in my gut as possible.

Rick was smiling when he returned. He looked satisfied and refreshed. I was nauseous and terrified.

"Come here," I said. I wrapped my body around him. I let him have all of me while I floated up out of myself and watched from the ceiling. I was doing what I had to do to keep him.

When Rick was gratified, he held me close and said, "You know just how to handle me."

"Have you done this before?" I said.

He sighed. "Yeah, I used to do it to Karen all the time."

This was news to me. "What would she do?"

"She would freak out and ignore me for days. She was so cold. Not like you."

I felt disgusted with myself. What had I become? I was with a man who was showing himself to be not only emotionally unavailable but also borderline abusive. No wonder he reminded me of my father at times. Rick wasn't physically abusive like my dad, but the pain he caused was just as bad, if not worse. Intellectually, I knew the intelligent thing to do was leave, but I felt powerless to go. I was so attached to Rick I believed I wouldn't survive if I left him.

I returned with Rick to Casper for Thanksgiving, this time with the consideration of possibly making it my new home. Everything in my mind said no to moving there, but everything in my heart said yes to making Rick happy. It was a pattern that had started with my father, repeated with Chris in college, and Karl in Germany. No one had taught me that loyalty doesn't mean taking unlimited pain from broken men.

Rick bought me a full winter wardrobe—coat, hat, gloves, and boots. He emptied dresser drawers for me and made space in the closet. I played Pokémon cards and put puzzles together with Simon for hours. Rick watched with joyful admiration. "It's like we're a real family," he said, kissing me on top of the head.

We ordered a full turkey dinner for the three of us. There were piles of meat, mashed potatoes, green beans, and dinner rolls. Rick put on the football game, and Simon played on the iPad. It was every fantasy that I'd ever had about living a "normal" life. I didn't have to work anymore. I didn't have to chase boats or boys or try to accomplish anything. All I had to do was be Rick's partner. Be good, be pleasant, be cool. We went to bed, stuffed with pie and pleasure. Snow fell lightly outside, and the dog snored softly in the corner. I felt like I was living in a snow globe, safe and warm and satiated.

A few hours later, Rick's phone rang and woke me. Karen had gotten drunk and swallowed a bottle of sleeping pills. She was in the hospital.

Rick went into full rescue mode. "I have to find a rehab for her," he said. "I need to get her help."

"You're not her family anymore," I reminded him. "She has a family. They can help her."

My serenity was darkened with emptiness and loneliness as Rick paced around the house. He made coffee. He Googled things and sent emails. My presence was irrelevant, my opinion inconsequential. I didn't know whether to pity Karen or resent her for the intrusion. I swallowed my feelings but I didn't know how much more I could take.

I flew back to California alone, got into bed, pulled the sheets over my head, and cried for hours. Rick organized an intervention and found a rehab for Karen. When he arrived in California a week later, I was still in bed. My emotions had turned to infection, and my body was hot with a fever. Rick made soup for me, and we took a walk. I rallied my strength and returned to the task of disassembling the business that I had created for Rick.

I moved through the following days with a kind of seasickness, reminiscent of the time when my father was dying. My sleep was restless. My body flooded with adrenaline as I waited for Rick to say that the sale was final.

I woke one morning, and Rick was checking his phone. "It's done," he said. Rick didn't look happy. He was even more worn and tattered than when we reconnected two years earlier.

I launched into a full-blown panic attack. I shook and hyperventilated as I fell into a black hole of emptiness.

"You're scaring me," Rick said. He grabbed his things and started to leave.

"Please don't leave me," I begged.

"This isn't working," he said.

This is all my fault, I thought. If I just move to Wyoming like he wants, if I concede and stop being so selfish, everything will be fine. "I'll come and stay with you. Please don't leave."

Rick shook his head, his eyes dark with rejection. "I don't want to take care of you."

"Everything will be okay. I promise." I was trauma bonded to him. I was addicted. Leaving him was unthinkable. I reached down deep inside myself to the strength that had gotten me through my dissertation, my yoga training, the death of two parents, and all my other challenges. I conjured the power of love, purpose, and passion that had fueled me to create the wellness retreats. I could do this. I couldn't give up. The following day, I applied for jobs in Casper.

To celebrate, Rick whisked me off on another trip—a seven-day Caribbean cruise. We frolicked in the turquoise waters of the Caribbean Sea and lounged by the pool with margaritas. We wandered the streets of San Juan, Puerto Rico, and climbed through the caves of Tortola. It felt like old times; like we were free at last from the year of friction and heartache.

Rick gave me another hand-written card. *I feel better than I have in years. I can finally be with you and give you what you deserve. Thank you so much for everything you have done for me. You are amazing. You are so beautiful. You are so damn smart. I am so lucky you remembered me and didn't ignore my email. I love you and love that you share your world with me. I can't wait for all the amazing adventures that we will have together.*

I read the words again and again. I was relieved and grateful. I forced the doubts and anxiety out of my head and chose to believe that all of the struggles were worthwhile if we could have a happy future together.

We returned to Casper after our trip and Rick organized a barbecue to introduce me to all the neighbors. We sat in the yard, eating hamburgers and drinking cold beer, while the kids frolicked in the blow-up pool. I felt safe and warm, drenched with relief that Rick and I were living together again. My stomach hurt all the time. I ignored it. I tried to shove down the knowing, but it kept coming back to the surface.

The next day, I sat with Rick in the kitchen, discussing our schedule and plans for the future. I thought we could get married and be a real family. Maybe I could do some consulting work in California and travel back and forth like some of his neighbors were doing.

When I told my ideas to Rick, his face got red and his hands got sweaty. He burst out in anger again. Even though this wasn't new behavior whenever I talked about our future together and I should have known better, I still felt shocked and confused.

I left the kitchen and went to the bedroom, where I sat on the closet floor and stared out the window. I stayed in the closet for a long time.

Rick found me and asked if I wanted to get a cup of coffee. We walked a few blocks to the cafe. It was quiet and awkward as we talked about the neighbor who cut down too many trees and caused all the other neighbors to come out and take pictures and post them on Facebook.

After we were seated at the café table, Rick said that he didn't want to be disrespectful with his reactiveness and defensiveness. It wasn't an apology. It was just a statement. Then he said something about not wanting deadlines, and how he'd worked hard in his twenties and thirties to have a stress-free future.

"I don't want any transactions with you," he said.

"Transactions?" I repeated in stunned disbelief. I felt so insignificant, like an object he kept around as long as it served him.

Rick shrugged. "I don't want to give you any assurances."

His words were devastating. I had given him everything; I had nothing left to give. I clenched every muscle in my body to hold in my anguish, and swallowed my tears. I didn't want to cry in front of Rick ever again.

While I slept, I traveled through other dimensions, a psychic trip into the web of our lives. I saw Rick's relationship with his mother, his disgust and frustration with her choices. I saw his relationship with his father, the terror, and the rage at his father's abandonment. I saw Rick's bond with his child. The energy of parenting. I saw my father in Rick's eyes, in his smile, and in his gestures when he cuddled Simon, fought with his ex, or looked at me through a fake smile. I saw the diamond ring and dozens of flowers my father gave me. I saw the way these men loved me, the way they feared me, the way it felt like it was never enough for any of us. I felt like we had been doing this dance for lifetimes, like our connection went way beyond this moment in time, lives overlapping lives overlapping lives.

Rick and I got on a plane to Los Angeles a few weeks later to celebrate our two-year anniversary. As we settled in for the flight he gave me another handwritten card expressing his appreciation for me.

I cannot believe it's been two years since you came back into my life. It feels like it was meant to be. You were exactly what I needed at exactly the right time. I hope that you feel the same way—that we were meant to be with each other, that when we first met over a decade ago we weren't ready, and that we would eventually reconnect, and it would be that once-in-a-lifetime love. I always want to be with you. You are everything I want, and you love me better and more than I could have ever imagined. Let's plan the rest of our adventures together. I am the luckiest man in the world.

Rick's words were always the perfect words, and words of affirmation were my love language. I wanted to believe his note more than anything in the world. Every cell of my being told me Rick was "the one." There was a physical, psychological, emotional, and spiritual resonance that made me feel like he was my person. I needed to have someone like him because I had so many unmet needs that left a hole the size of the Grand Canyon in my heart. I had the need for security and safety, which unconsciously I learned could only come from a man.

Even though I had been working on female empowerment and self-sufficiency for two decades, it was the belief that a man with money could take much better care of me than I could take of myself that was deeply ingrained in me.

I had the need for intimacy and affection. We all have needs for human connection. If our abuser is meeting those needs, we may become attached to them in an unhealthy way. Hostages can even develop a bond with their captors during captivity. This phenomenon is called Stockholm Syndrome, after four hostages who fell in love with their kidnappers.

Most of all, I had a need to be part of a family. My parents were dead, I was estranged from my siblings, and it had been more than 40 years since I felt a sense of family bliss. The more time I spent on holidays and other visits with Rick's child, parents, and extended family, the more I felt the hole in my heart filling up with love. I was not ready to quit. I kept telling myself that I could make it better, that we could figure it out. I believed that I needed him, and he needed me, and that loving harder was more important than giving up.

We were seated side-by-side, my arm wrapped around Rick's. He was watching a video, and I was looking around the plane. I saw businessmen, a family of four with a restless child, sun-kissed girls taking selfies and giggling.

Just then, the quiet voice in my mind broke through the silence. *Life could completely change in an instant.* It sounded ominous, like an oracle's prediction of tragedy.

Oh no, I silently answered. *Don't do this. Please don't take him away from me.* I imagined that the plane could crash, and everyone on it would face an entirely different future than the one they had right now.

I squeezed Rick's hand and said, "I don't know what would happen to me if something happened to you."

He looked at me, puzzled, and returned to watching his movie.

We checked into an Airbnb in Venice Beach. I was looking forward to a relaxing weekend with our friends, hopeful that this escape would be just the medicine that we needed to reconnect. I blamed stress for so much of our conflict—the stress of Rick's divorce, his custody battle, his business, his health. Maybe without the stress, things would be smooth sailing.

We walked a few blocks to an Italian restaurant where we ordered pasta and wine and had an easy conversation. Rick seemed detached at dinner, with a faraway, distracted look. I didn't know if he was unhappy or maybe his blood sugar was low. I tried not to make up stories in my head. We finished the meal and went outside to the curb. He seemed spacey, like he was drunk. But he'd had just one glass of wine.

His sugar must be low. I started to panic. I called an Uber and tried to get us back to the room as fast as possible.

In the room, Rick's monitor said his blood sugar was dangerously low. I panicked more. I had never seen him have a diabetic reaction, but I had heard horror stories from him and his mother of sweating, shaking, passing out. I might be responsible for his life if he couldn't take care of himself. I forced him to have some sugar. He was getting annoyed with me. We went out in search of sugary drinks. He grew more irritated with me. No matter how much sugar he had, his monitor still said he was dangerously low. I was shaking all over.

I texted his mom and his best friend, saying, "I don't want to freak out, but Rick's monitor says his sugar is low, and it's not coming back up."

They both responded that this was an emergency. I needed to call 911. Rick was livid. He grabbed his things and tried to run away.

"You are hysterical," he shouted. "Get away from me. I never want to see you again."

Terrified that he would leave and die in the street, I stood in front of the door, trying to block his escape.

He grabbed my arm and pushed me out of the way.

"Don't touch me," I yelled. My head was spinning. My heart pounded.

I remembered the voice from the plane, *Life could completely change in an instant.*

This is it. This is where I lose him.

I followed Rick into an Uber and we went to his friend's house. His friend consoled me. Rick's mom called and reassured me that everything would be ok. Rick wouldn't make eye contact with me. The three of us walked to the pharmacy to get another monitor. It said that his blood sugar was higher than normal, but in a safe range.

We returned to his friends' house. Rick turned to me. "Get out, Gabby," He said coldly.

"It's okay," his friend said. "I'll take care of him. You should go back to your place and get some rest."

I was baffled. I felt hurt, overwhelmed and terrified. Rick wanted nothing to do with me. I returned to the room alone. I couldn't sleep. My whole body burned. My life was unraveling.

At six the next morning, I texted Rick and begged him to return. He ignored me.

At eight, I got in an Uber and went back to his friend's house. Rick was in the driveway with his suitcase, waiting for a taxi.

"Where are you going?" I asked.

"I'm going to a hotel. Why are you here?"

He wasn't going to come back to me. I couldn't see straight or think straight. I couldn't even feel my body.

"I'm not safe," I pleaded. "Please don't leave me alone."

"I want you out of my life. This is too complicated. Tell me where you want me to send your things."

The air left my body. My heart clenched and my head imploded. How could Rick throw me out on the street like a bag of garbage?

I dug deep and reached for my strength. Silently I asked the Universe, *What should I do? Please tell me what to do!*

Walk away.

A raw and wild freedom rushed into my legs and carried me away. I watched in slow motion as the trees and houses went by. Rick faded into the ethers. As the sun descended beneath the watery pink and orange horizon, the previous two years of California light gently faded to black.

17

THERE IS A SAYING in addiction recovery, "You're only as sick as your secrets." If you want to convince other people something didn't happen, the best way is to convince yourself first. I managed to arrive at 45 years of age believing nothing "that bad" happened to me. I had walled off certain thoughts and emotions related to my secrets that not only blocked my connection to others, but also made me vulnerable to the worst kind of manipulations.

My secrets were ugly. They were forbidden. And I was sure beyond a shadow of a doubt that if anyone heard them, they would never want to be close to me again.

They say confronting your secrets is the first step in being honest with yourself. And that exposing your secrets to the light takes away their power and relieves you of their burden. What they don't say is that secrets will do everything in their power to remain secrets. You may have to shatter your entire life to release them. Cracks, after all, are where the light gets in.

A few days after I left Rick in the summer of 2019 I stood naked in the shower, cold water rushing over me, my whole body shaking. Tears streamed down my face. I had woken up in a panic, gasping for breath.

A supernatural force had started moving through me during the night, pushing submerged memories to the surface and bringing every emotion to the forefront. Whatever pain had been frozen inside of me was melting. Whatever trauma had been blocked was pouring out. I had woken up burning like I was submerged in lava, as if kerosene was running through my veins, and someone had lit a match to my nervous system.

The cold shower wasn't helping much. I was freezing on the outside and burning on the inside as my whole life flashed before my eyes.

I must be dying. No one could survive this.

I had been sleeping on an air mattress on my friend's apartment floor for a few nights. While my friend was at work, I walked up and down the dirt hills of Runyon Canyon, panting, crying, and listening to *Women Who Love Too Much* repeatedly on my headphones.

Loving an abusive partner is so complex it took me years to peel back all the layers of my psyche and figure out what was going on, but the book helped me learn about the dynamics. On the most fundamental level, if our partner makes us feel the same as our primary caregivers, our mind and body will register it as not only familiar, but also call it "love." When we find someone who matches our primary caregiver's personality, it feels like the perfect fit, even if the fit is toxic. The unconditional love that we had for our parents transfers to the person who most reminds us of them, resulting in a trauma bond and dependency that feels necessary for survival.

But we can't see any of this because it is hidden from our view. It's buried in a part of our mind called the "shadow," which means exactly what it sounds like. Our psychological shadow, the haunted house of our psyche, is where we store our abuse and neglect. It operates unconsciously in our life until it's integrated.

We all have a need for our inner and outer worlds to be consistent and congruent. When we act perfect on the outside but our insides are a mess, the shadow will manifest in unhealthy habits and patterns—like overeating or emotional outbursts—until we find a way to acknowledge—and even love- the most unlovable parts of ourselves.

When we store low self-esteem in our shadow, we unconsciously attract partners who treat us badly because, even though we pretend to feel worthy, our inner self feels worthless. If someone is respectful to us, it can be much harder to accept because it challenges all of our assumptions and beliefs about ourselves.

If we don't have a loving relationship with ourselves, we can't handle someone else loving us unconditionally. Without unlearning those patterns and relearning new healthy ones, we're destined to repeat the patterns indefinitely.

I could finally glimpse the dysfunctional patterns and recognize the ways I wasn't being truly seen or heard in my life. How I had repeatedly abandoned myself, avoided loving myself, poured myself into work or appearance or relationships so that I would be valued and appreciated. I grieved the way I had repeatedly given away my power and abused myself with unkind words.

How did I not see this before? Why did I have to go through something so hurtful to uncover all of this?

The burning lasted for a few hours, and then a few days. Then I couldn't make it stop. I felt like I had as a child—like a soda can that had been shaken so hard for so long that I could barely contain the compression anymore.

I reached out to my friend Michelle, the one who I'd worked with in the rehabs. She was a psychotherapist in Los Angeles now.

When I told her about the fallout with Rick, she listened compassionately and then spoke honestly.

"You've come too far to end up in an abusive relationship," she said. "You need to do the work that you tell everyone else to do. You don't want to be a hypocrite, do you?"

The word "hypocrite" reverberated in my mind, piercing through the armor of illusion that I was fine. Other people had addictions and illness. I was a Ph.D. professor. I had my shit together.

It was Dad, or Mom, or my brother, or Rick, that needed help, not me. I had tried so many treatments and practices for my lifelong headaches, panic attacks, burning ulcers, and bursting cysts, but I had never really gotten to the source. Never pulled the trauma out by the roots. Never told anyone my secrets. I suspected I had to confront the baggage of the past to create the future that I wanted, but I hadn't the faintest clue where to begin.

"You should go to the Meadows' Survivors Workshop in Arizona," Michelle said.

"Okay," I said, desperate for relief.

"You might die," she joked. "Seriously, it's the hardest thing you'll ever do in your life."

"Sounds like fun," I deadpanned.

I felt like I had no choice. I had been living a false life for so long, obsessed with pleasing others, chasing happiness, desperate for distraction and escape. There was nowhere left to go, nothing left to do, except face the pain head-on. Even if it killed me.

When I arrived at the ranch in the Arizona desert, it felt like this reckoning was a long time coming. Every bad relationship, every self-destructive behavior, and every addictive pattern had led to this moment. I could run no more.

According to The Meadows' website, I would enjoy five days and four nights exploring "childhood wounding," and, "releasing the negative messages and emotions that were rooted in painful experiences from the past."

Spending a week immersed in my childhood memories sounded like torture. I hated my past with a passion. I had been avoiding it since I sat on Dr. Kelly's couch in the 1990s.

I gathered with a dozen people inside the modest lobby to listen to the welcome talk. There were folding chairs and therapy books stacked on various tables and shelves around the room. I could see a patch of wildflowers outside the window. The woman at the podium had the cautious tone of a whitewater rafting guide, warning us that the rapids might drown us without actually saying as much. At least, that's how I heard it.

The beautiful girl next to me, a famous actress who I recognized immediately, whispered, "I've heard the experiential part is mental."

"Really?" I replied.

"Yeah. My friend did this workshop last month, and she told me it was bloody hard."

"Oh God." My empty stomach churned.

After the talk, we gathered in two rooms in small groups of six people each and shared more intimate introductions. Whiteboards hung side by side on the front wall, with inspirational sayings written in erasable marker. There was a basket of stuffed animals, and foam bats, and a suspicious number of tissue boxes stacked in the corner.

I sat in one of the chairs, organized in a half-moon formation. To my left was Wendy, a twenty-something girl who worked at the ranch. She was bitterly self-conscious about the extra one-hundred pounds she carried on her body. To my right was Mary, a tiny British girl who was recovering from her mother's suicide earlier in the year. Across from me was Emily, actress from the welcome talk. Bridget, an adulterous nurse, was attending the program to try and save her marriage. All of these women had a prescription to be there—a psychiatrist or marriage counselor had advised them to attend. I was there because I was receiving no care, not from a doctor or counselor, not even from myself.

Our fearless leader, Dr. Maya, sat facing us, her back to the whiteboards. She had olive skin and short dark hair. I knew from her bio on the website that she had been saving inner children for decades. The embodiment of all of the qualities of a righteous female warrior, she reminded me of the fierce detective Olivia Benson on Law & Order.

In her overview of the program, Dr. Maya told us that we needed to let go and trust her. Even if we didn't understand the methods or couldn't stomach the techniques, we needed to surrender and let her take control.

"Your best thinking got you here," she said, "Only new thinking will get you out."

I felt a mixture of revulsion and relief. I craved a confident guide who could tell me exactly what to do and how to do it. I yearned to put my life in her hands. I also resisted the idea of surrender. I was terrified that she would drop me like so many others whom I had trusted.

The reality, though, was that I was so low, even if she dropped me, there was not very far to fall. I decided that all my efforts had gotten me as far as the front door of the Meadows. I needed Dr. Maya to get me across to the other side of my trauma, once and for all.

After she gave an overview of the program and handed out reading materials, Dr. Maya dismissed us with the warning that we would be spending long days together for the rest of the week. She forbade us from using phones, computers, or having any contact with the outside world. It was not much of a sacrifice for me. There was no one and nothing I really wanted in that moment, anyway.

Instead, Dr. Maya said we had some serious homework we needed to complete before we returned the next morning. We had to chronicle the abuses of our childhood on paper with names, dates, and categories. Trauma could be physical, mental, emotional, spiritual, or sexual.

I gawked at the paper in horror. This was the worst possible assignment in the world. It was just like Dr. Gordon's genogram that had caused me to have a panic attack a decade earlier, only worse. This time, I not only had to talk about my family, I had to reveal all the secrets, too.

I was in a daze as I walked back to my cabin in the fading afternoon light. The air was dry, and a light coat of coral-colored dust covered the stone path. Little lizards scurried by my feet. A jackrabbit bounced nearby under a bush. If I wasn't at a rehab center, it would have been beautiful.

Inside the cabin, I sat at the small desk and with a shaky hand, began to write my story.

At three years old I was a tiny little thing who loved to wear Mickey Mouse ears and rhinestone tiaras. I was always putting on some kind of performance in the living room, usually in front of the TV. I had a crew of puppets and stuffed animals, and sometimes I would drag my baby brother into the scene as my sidekick or live audience member. Joy wrapped around me like a warm blanket. I knew nothing of winter, even when I was swaddled in puffy snowsuits, riding a toboggan down the icy hills of Hershey, Pennsylvania.

One day, in the midst of a living-room dance routine, I heard raised voices in the kitchen and moved closer to see what was happening.

Mom and Dad were face to face, arguing about something. It was the first time I had seen them this way. Unafraid, I moved even closer. I could feel the heat rising in the room like someone had turned up the furnace. The voices rose too, with increasing intensity and fury. Hands waved above my head. I tightened my legs. My feet froze to the ground. Then something ignited in Dad. He cocked his thick arm back and punched Mom in the face. I could hear the CRACK upon impact. I locked my spindly arms around Dad's leg, hoping to pull him away. He kicked me off while reaching for a fistful of Mom's hair.

That's when Mom saw me. Her baby blue eyes were red. "Oh my God," she said. "Oh my God. Oh my God. Oh my God." She picked me up from the floor, carried me into the bathroom, and locked the door.

With one hand she undressed me, and with the other, she filled the tub with water. I was shivering and gasping for breath. She picked me up and plopped me into the tub. The water did nothing to soothe me. I was inconsolable.

At first, my mother was sympathetic. She caressed me with a warm wash cloth. When my tears wouldn't stop flowing, she became enraged. "Knock it off," she snapped, "Stop being so dramatic."

A jolt of terror shocked me. I froze like a frightened animal. I was no longer safe in the world.

I threw the pen across the room and started to hyperventilate. I could feel the lukewarm water on my skin. I could feel my mother's hands on me. I wanted to scream. I wanted to punch my fist through the perfect fucking cabin window.

I had not even been at the workshop for a full day and I was already coming undone. Who was I kidding?

I'll never survive 5 days of this.

My emotion was too much for my mother. It was too much for me, too. There had always been too many feelings and nowhere to put them.

I thought of Rick and the breakup, and how he discarded me like trash. I shook and I cried. I debated with myself for a long time. I tried to come up with excuses to leave. I heard Michelle in my head, saying *Don't be a hypocrite.* I decided I wasn't going down without a fight.

Let's go, motherfucker. This is only the beginning,

I walked across the room, picked up the pen, and started writing again.

It was the late 1970s, and the burn of my parent's first fight faded into long days of summer—carousel rides at Hersheypark and silver-wrapped Kisses. I sat on Dad's shoulders, my fingers buried in his curly black hair, feeling like a princess on her chariot.

I rode that feeling all the way to Scranton, where my world expanded from four rooms to fourteen rooms as we crossed the threshold of an old Victorian house. I ran up and down the stairs, opening every door and cabinet, looking for secret passageways and ancient treasures. The house contained creaking steps, peeling wallpaper, and something ominous in the attic.

I felt like the captain of a magnificent pirate ship about to embark on a great adventure. Dad showed off his fatherly skills by building us a treehouse and tire swing in the backyard. He even got us a racing go-kart that was the envy of the entire neighborhood. Mom was busy fixing the house into a perfect fairytale castle.

It wasn't long before our house simmered with raised voices and dangerous conversations again. Mom and Dad had a room above mine, and each thump made me freeze a little. One night, after a flare-up, Mom tumbled down the stairs and into my room. She was sweaty and scared and crawled into bed between my brother and me.

Dad, a dark silhouette in the doorway, called my name, "Gabrielle."

I pretended not to hear.

"Gabrielle," he insisted. I crawled out of bed and followed him to the guest bedroom across the hallway.

He sat on the edge of the bed so that we were eye to eye. At seven years old I was half his height. He looked big and broken, and there were lots of words and tears that I didn't understand. A cold heat moved through my limbs, my nightgown sticky on my skin.

Finally, I heard something that I understood. He said, "I am going to cut up your mother with a butcher knife and bury her in the backyard."

I saw an image of my mother dropped into dirt holes, piece by piece. I saw the lumpy yard where our playground was supposed to be. I couldn't blink or breathe. I didn't know what to say.

My father pulled me close and squeezed me tight. He smelled like alcohol and aftershave. He seemed relieved and unburdened.

And then he sent me back to bed.

I dropped the pen, stood up and braced myself against the wall. Choking sobs filled my throat. I remembered the nightmares which began that night and stayed with me for decades. I remembered enveloping darkness and how the house, which used to be so beautiful and magical, smelled like evil and rotting corpses. I remembered the way that my whole being felt cracked, and how shame spread like a spider web across my life. I had no one to tell and no way to explain it. I wept for myself, for all the pain and regret, for the little girl who lost her childhood in a situation she couldn't escape. For the secrets I carried for so long, for the damage they caused to my mind and body.

The grief turned to rage that turned to heat, which made me angrier than I've ever been. I picked up the pen and started writing again.

Some nights were quiet, and I would fall asleep peacefully with my cat curled at my feet. Sometimes Mom would tuck me in with a lullaby. On the nights when the rumbling started just after dark, I would lie with eyes wide open, waiting for the explosion.

One night, when I was 8 years old, Mom's screams became too loud to ignore. I stuffed my brother in a closet and then tiptoed downstairs to the phone and dialed 911.

"My dad is hitting my mom," I said.

I could see the red and blue lights flooding the kitchen before I heard the knock at the door. I crept into the darkness behind the stairs as Dad stumbled toward the men in black. Mom had crawled under a table and was whimpering and covering her face with her hands.

I heard the men say, "Ma'am, do you want to press charges?"

Mom said, "No."

"Ma'am, there is nothing we can do if you don't press charges," the officers warned.

"No."

"Ma'am, we really think you would be safer if—"

"No."

I heard footsteps moving toward the door. I watched as the red and blue lights faded to black.

The tears felt warm on my cheeks. I blew my nose fiercely and kept writing until the sky turned from pastel pink to navy blue to black. I knew my inner girl had absorbed this trauma like she absorbed everything else. She thought being frozen was better than feeling the constant heat and agonizing burn. If she were frozen, she could ignore the things that were really going on. She could ignore that unicorns weren't real, and the understanding that families like hers would never be fixed. She could ignore that she felt lonely and hungry and terrified all the time. Being frozen made her feel less of everything.

Now, I was thawing her out. It was going to hurt. A lot.

I was conjuring ghosts. I knew they had been haunting me for a long time, but I had no idea what was going to happen next. I was scared to stop writing and get into bed for fear of what might attack me in my sleep.

The next morning when I arrived in the group therapy session, Dr. Maya looked down at the crumpled paper where I had written about Mom and Dad. It read like a sort of police report, although no one had been caught or convicted. One by one, she read off the incidents and ask me to explain them.

I felt paralyzed. I had never walked through this story with anyone before. I could feel the eyes of the five other women on me.

They will think I am a freak. The humiliation will kill me.

"I don't think it's safe," I said.

"Safe for who?" Dr. Maya asked.

"For them," I said, gesturing to the others. "I don't think it's safe for them to be in the room right now."

I was genuinely concerned for the other women. I thought that my secrets had so much power that just hearing them would wreak havoc on their lives. I was sure they would be traumatized by my trauma.

"We can handle it," Dr. Maya assured. "Go ahead."

I stared at her in disbelief. I could feel the sweat collecting in my palms and my armpits. I closed my eyes and opened my mouth.

"I was three years old the first time my father tried to kill my mother," I said, then faltered. I looked up at Dr. Maya.

"Keep going," she encouraged.

We were off on a voyage across a wicked sea. I gripped the arms of the chair as the room lurched and rolled in every direction. Shame and pain pounded and slammed my body.

"I tried to defend her. I put myself between them. I tried to stop it. I couldn't stop it. I could never stop it."

"You were three years old," Dr. Maya gently reminded me. "It wasn't your job to stop it. It was your job to be a child. It was their job to protect you."

I shook in my chair, clenching my fists so hard that my forearms cramped. I was saying something so bold, so forbidden, that I feared the impact of the words would break all of us into pieces.

"How does that make you feel?" Dr. Maya asked when I finished sharing what I had written.

"Like I'm on fire. Like I'm burning alive."

Dr. Maya nodded. "That's pain. Where do you feel it?"

"Everywhere. Everything is burning."

She nodded again. "That's a lot of pain."

The room swirled and swayed. I felt the battering of memories, emotions, and nightmares like a harrowing storm. The past and present rushed together, a swirl of raucous winds.

"Keep going," Dr. Maya said.

I wasn't sure I could keep going. My mind vacillated between resistance and persistence, rapidly bouncing back and forth like a tennis match. I had no good reasons to quit and one compelling reason to keep going. I wanted to save my own life.

I had to let go and trust her.

I took a deep breath and then blurted out, "He kicked the cat, and then there was a big lump on its head." I paused and then added more softly, "And then it was *dead.*"

I squeezed my eyes hard. Tears rained down my blouse. "I buried it in the yard. I covered it with dirt...

"WHO DOES THAT?" My voice climbed to a scream. "Who gives you a kitten and then kills it? Why would anyone do that?"

Dr. Maya let me wail and then encouraged me to keep going.

I was dripping with sweat and snot as I recounted the night when I was 8 years old and I woke abruptly to the wail of sirens. The familiar red and blue lights blinked through my bedroom window. I crawled down to the dark space behind the kitchen stairs. Mom scrambled through the door, hair stuck to her face, black mascara running down her cheeks. She looked like an animal being chased.

I held my breath and listened hard. I heard Mom tell the babysitter, "He tried to shoot me."

"What? Are you okay?" The babysitter sounded frightened.

"He missed. He shot the back window of the car."

Mom grabbed bags from the closet and stuffed things into them like a crazed robber.

I went back to my bed, crawled under my blankets, and lay absolutely still.

Mom came in a few seconds later. "Hurry up! Get dressed!" she said.

She went into my brother's room and I heard her say, "Wake up, honey, wake up. We have to go."

I grabbed a few things that I couldn't live without—a stuffed bear, my pink diary, a purple jacket.

Mom came back into my room and reached for my hand. It was strong and bony, with long scratchy fingernails. My brother was wrapped around her like a baby monkey. I slipped as we hurried down the stairs. Mom yanked my arm, pulled us together, and snapped at me, "Be careful!"

As we drove away from the house, I wondered if my father would chase us. I wondered if he would catch us. I wondered what would happen if he did.

"How does that make you feel?" Dr. Maya said.

"My stomach." I doubled over from the sensation. "It feels like some-one is kicking me in the stomach."

"Good," Dr. Maya said. She laid a hand on mine and looked me in the eyes. "Your parents didn't protect you. The police didn't protect you. *No one* protected you. Your father was a homicidal maniac. He should have been in jail."

He should have been in jail.

It was the best thing that anyone had ever said to me about my father.

And I fucking loved her for it.

An hour later, after recounting every incident from my dad hanging my brother over Niagara Falls to Mom's sudden and tragic death, the room gently steadied, as if the sea was calm. For a brief and cool mo-ment, I stepped across a threshold to an expansive space where I was not the one to blame for what had happened. It was not my responsibility to fix it. It was not my shame to carry, nor my guilt to bear.

Dr. Maya congratulated me on persevering through the pain. She had intentionally triggered me and forced me to break through every frozen trauma in my being. I felt like I had walked across coals of fire, unburned and victorious. I didn't realize until months later the grace and skill required for Dr. Maya to rebirth me in that room, to pull me through the perilous darkness into the light without causing further harm. She had not only performed a sort of miracle that day by releasing my past, but she gave me an unfamiliar faith in myself—a belief that I was stronger than the things that happened to me. I knew if I could walk through fire in that room, I could survive anything I faced when I walked out the door.

During the next few days, each of the girls took their turns in the hot seat with Dr. Maya. I sat in the chair closest to the door. I watched and listened as Dr. Maya took each of the participants through peeling back layers of psychic skin, exposing their most private parts as they struggled to tell their stories. I writhed in my seat with empathic pain. I wanted to defend, comfort, rescue, soothe, save them from the hurt, but the therapy room was a "no help" zone. No healing. No teaching. No fixing. Nobody to take care of but myself.

When we ended the session for dinner, I staggered into the dining room, feeling weak and exhausted. Several round wooden tables, mostly empty, and a buffet of freshly prepared food awaited us. I had no appetite but I gathered soup and salad mechanically and sat with my four brave companions near the sliding glass door. Other patients and therapists settled into the tables around us. There was a low hum of conversation. We didn't talk about the battle taking place behind the therapy doors. Instead, we chatted about movies, and books, and places we had traveled. I smiled politely, the shockwaves of the workshop still pulsing in my nerves.

The following days blurred into one long session of lessons and confessions. Dr. Maya educated us about the neuroscience of trauma and the origins of self-defeating behaviors such as addictions, mood disorders, and abusive relationships. She explained that children who froze as a response to emotional or physical abuse develop a tendency toward disassociation, panic disorders, and PTSD. It was all starting to make sense. My trauma caused me to freeze, which caused me to be anxious, which led to running away from things I needed to address. She explained that ultimately the best way to avoid more pain is to heal the underlying trauma, which helps remove or lessen the triggers. This would help me feel more stable and safer in the world.

Dr. Maya referenced codependency, attachment styles, trauma bonds, and the inner child. Each concept was already stored in the electronic files of my brain from a lifetime immersion in psychology literature. I understood them in the way that I understood a country that I had seen in a book but had never actually visited. I was finally getting some first-hand experience, something tangible I could build on. Even though I had a Ph.D., I knew I was taking my first steps on an entirely different learning journey. Dr. Maya gave me some basic tools I needed, namely radical honesty and self-responsibility, but I was still a work in progress. I knew I was going to have to take the seeds she'd planted and re-grow myself from the ground up.

"The next phase of the workshop will be experiential," Dr. Maya explained one afternoon. "We're going to hold your caregivers accountable for the ways that you were shamed, neglected, or abused. Then we will begin the reparenting process. It's going to be more challenging than what we've done so far but as long as you follow my instructions, you will be fine. In my wildest imagination, I couldn't imagine how the "bootcamp" could get any harder. I felt like I had scaled the walls, rolled under the barbed wire, and run through the flames. What else could we possibly do?

"The first line should be, 'I am holding you accountable for...'" Dr. Maya said. Accountability was different than blame. Accountability acknowledged that maybe they were doing their best. Maybe they didn't have bad intentions.

But accountability was also holding the offenders responsible for their actions, regardless of their intentions. It was returning carried shame to the rightful owner and declaring the damage that was done out loud, regardless of reasoning.

The thought of audibly addressing my parents for their discretions made me weak in the knees, but I wanted to tell the truth more than anything I had ever wanted in my life. I wanted others to know the truth. And I wanted them to believe me. I had spent too long thinking I was crazy and trying to win the affections of people who didn't deserve me. I wanted to be free. I wanted to be seen and accepted for who I really was, wounds and all, and it felt more urgent than a ticking time bomb.

Dr. Maya sat across from me and had me address her as if she was my mother.

"I am holding you accountable for not protecting me," I began in a wobbly voice that grew stronger as I went on. "I'm holding you accountable for sleeping for days and going out with strange men." I told one truth after another. I told her what I needed and didn't get. I told her what I got and didn't want.

Sometimes, my whole body would lock, my voice box would turn off, and I would float above the chair. "I can't feel my body," I said.

"Okay, look around the room. Look for colors. Find something red. Find something blue," Dr. Maya said.

The room held many random objects. I forced myself to focus on the colors. Anne was wearing red shoes. A blue book sat on the shelf.

I looked back at Dr. Maya and made eye contact with her.

"Nice job," she said. "You got this. Now, look at the other women."

One by one, I connected with the faces of the other girls. I saw unconditional compassion reflected back at me. A lightness of being entered my body, like the weight of judgment had been lifted. I bit my tongue to hold back the tears.

"Okay," said Dr. Maya. "Now we are going to invite your father into the room."

I was lightheaded and disoriented. I had stepped into a long, dark passage, and I still couldn't see the light at the other end. I had avoided this tunnel all of my life. I felt the magnetic pull of the shadows and a vortex of dark energy daring me to engage.

"You ready?" Dr. Maya asked.

"Uh, huh," I mumbled.

The ghost of Dad walked into the room and sat in the chair across from me. My vision blurred. My heart pounded. Fear flooded my body so fully that I felt like I was falling out of an airplane.

Dad was kicking Mom like a dog on the floor. She was peeing on herself and howling, "I'm dying."

My mind was spinning. I was so dizzy I couldn't see straight. I had nothing to hold onto. I was immediately transported back in time, to the days after the divorce when Mom forced us to visit our father. I recounted for Dr. Maya and the others how I remembered him looking into my eyes, pleading with me.

"You know that I hit your mother because she says that you're bad, right? I'm doing it to protect you. No one talks about my little princess like that."

I wanted to believe him. I wanted to be his little princess, but it felt like a giant hand was gripping me, squeezing the life out of me. I knew that I wasn't always a good girl. I didn't know why he was hurting Mom because of me. I couldn't move my head to nod or acknowledge him.

"Your mom is a slut, and she's crazy," he insisted.

Dad squeezed me in his sweaty arms. I felt like I was being smothered by something invisible. I tried to ignore him, but his words crawled inside of me. He tucked the covers around me and walked toward the door. Before he turned off the light, he stopped and said, "I love you. You know you'll always be Daddy's little girl."

Now!" Dr. Maya shouted. "I am holding you accountable for—"

I was in so much pain I let out a yelp like I had just been shot. I shook my head from side to side, trying to toss the memories from my skull. Small bursts of nerve pain flared on my arms and legs, like flecks of sparkler fire, popping under my skin.

"I am holding you accountable for..." Dr. Maya repeated.

I held my breath and clenched my fists.

I heard a whisper, *The light at the end of the tunnel is not an illusion. The tunnel is.*

"I am holding you accountable for trying to kill my mother," I squeaked out.

"No," I corrected myself, my voice growing stronger, "I am holding you accountable for killing my mother."

When the confrontation was complete, Dr. Maya asked, "How are you feeling?"

I dropped into my heart. It felt like a fractured bone, tender and fragile. "Sad. I feel sad."

Dr. Maya nodded. "Good. Where do you feel it?"

I put my hand on my chest. "Here." The gesture required no explanation.

It felt like layers of clay were cracking off my shell, and more of my tenderness was being exposed. I could feel my heart, my needs, my Self—maybe for the first time ever. Underneath all of the grasping and scheming, posturing and pretending, I was finally getting in touch with my "being." I had the sense that she was young and sweet and didn't deserve any of the childhood cruelty. It also seemed like so much of the baggage I'd collected was not my own, but rather some generational garbage that had been passed on to me.

I'm giving it back, I thought. This is not my shit to carry.

On the last days of the workshop, we went on a mission to rescue our inner children. Dr. Maya took us back in time, via regression hypnosis, to find our inner children and bring them to safety. One by one, I watched and listened as Dr. Maya took the other girls on a journey. She guided Wendy back to her 10-year-old self, who was fat-shamed by her parents. She helped Mary escape from the unwanted sexual attention she received when she was 12. With Emily and Bridget, Dr. Maya saved them from being bullied in school. Then she returned with Mary to her mother's suicide when Mary was 14 and forged a new path forward.

Dr. Maya saved my rescue for last. We were not only going back to childhood, we were going back to the womb.

She asked me to close my eyes and envision August 1, 1974, my birthday.

In my mind's eye, I walked into the sterile delivery room in Hershey, PA. The air was humid and chaotic. Masked doctors and nurses surrounded my mother's bed. I could see my mother's agony and my father's expectation. I could feel the tension between them, her neediness and his indifference to her needs. I didn't want to be born to these people, which may have explained the 18 hours of labor. I wanted to leave the planet before I arrived. I was fighting and burning before I even came out of the womb.

As I was slipping into the world, my father reached for me. I felt a surge of adrenaline. There was no fucking way he was touching me. In a swift and sudden movement, my adult self reached in front of him, grabbed my bloody newborn self, and walked right out of the room. I swaddled her against my chest, felt the warmth of her breath and the beating of her heart. She was precious. She was perfect. She was an unbroken beautiful little girl. And she was mine.

Before I left the Survivors Workshop, Dr. Maya said that it would take a minimum of six months to integrate our experience. She warned that we had taken a big step, but still needed to do the challenging work of trauma recovery. I felt the bootcamp had purged me on the deepest level, and tore off the blind spots that had been blocking my true vision for so long.

I had been on a journey for more than 40 years, accumulating misguided learning about all kinds of things, from being a good Catholic girl to being a professional woman who fit into a neatly labeled box. It had been more than 20 years since the mystical experience at Mom's funeral and the beginning of my desperate pursuit of purpose, mission and meaning.

I had looked for love in all the wrong places, especially in romantic partners who hurt me. I had been searching all my life for someone outside myself to tell me how to be an adult, how to be a healer, how to be one-half of a happy couple.

What I really needed was less "doing" and more "being." I didn't need to "become" someone special; I was already someone authentically unique and irreplaceable. What I needed to do next, was forget the misguided thinking and start the process of returning to my natural state.

As I walked out of the Meadows Ranch, I noticed a purple amaranth pushing up through a crack in the sidewalk.

Now I could hear new voices, ones I hadn't heard before. If we could hear the consciousness of the flower, what would she say? If we acted less like conditioned humans and more like nature, how would we live differently?

I saw the flower as my stubborn, persistent, natural desire to reach, to grow, to grasp for air, water, and light. She was my color, my scent, my organic, evolving nature. She reminded me of my essence, and my reflection of everything in the natural world.

The concrete beneath my feet was my conditioned beliefs about right and wrong, good and bad. It was my stigmas and prejudices about myself, my family and my planet. It was my lifelong indoctrination as a member of a sick and violent culture.

Wholeness was not going to come from a prescription or a Ph.D. It was going to emerge from the dirt beneath my feet, like a lotus from the mud. I needed to reorient myself to live in attunement with the earth, to create from a place of alignment with her. No longer separate, but one unbroken fabric of connectedness.

As I pulled out onto the Arizona highway, most of the burning in my body was replaced by an expansive, soothing void. I didn't have my usual urgency or panic. Behind me, in the rear-view mirror, was the girl who thought she was broken, who believed she was never good enough, who thought that if anyone heard her secrets, they would never want to be close to her again.

Ahead of me shimmered a dream, emerging in the heat waves over the highway. I felt called to go on a new journey into nature, to reconnect with the eternally fruitful source of everything, Mother Earth. I didn't know it yet, but the path ahead would take me to misty volcanic mountains, Mayan ceremonies, and indigenous plant rituals, where shamans would open portals, soften my heart, and flood me with new life.

But in that moment, before the next adventure materialized, there was nothing but me, the road, and my inner baby girl riding shotgun. I didn't know where I was headed or what I was going to do, but I was eager and willing to step into the unknown—and find the light once again.

Ingram Content Group UK Ltd.
Milton Keynes UK
UKHW020627100323
418360UK00012B/1084